Arabic Short Stories for Complete Beginners

30 Exciting Short Stories to Learn Arabic & Grow Your Vocabulary the Fun Way

@All rights reserved 2019
Frédéric BIBARD (MyDailyArabic.com)

No part of this book including the audio material may be copied, reproduced, transmitted or distributed in any form without prior written permission of the author. For permission requests, write to: Frédéric BIBARD at contact@mydailyarabic.com.

For more products by Frédéric BIBARD, visit https://www.amazon.com/Frederic-BIBARD (for US)

https://www.amazon.co.uk/Frederic-BIBARD (for UK)

or go to https://mydailyarabic.com.

Table of Contents

مقدمة 7

Introduction 7

تريد نسخة غر يدوية؟ 9

Want The Hands-Free Version? 9

القصة ١ : اليوم الأول – الجزء ١ .... ١٠

Story 1 : First Day - Part 1 10

القصة الثانية : اليوم الأول – الجزء الثاني ١٢

Story 2 : First Day - Part 2 12

القصة ٣ : اليوم الأول-الجزء الثالث ١٤

Story 3 : First Day - Part 3 14

القصة ٤ : الذهاب في عطلة – الجزء الأول ١٦

Story 4 : Going On Holiday – Part 1 16

القصة ٥ : الذهاب في عطلة – الجزء الثاني ١٨

Story 5 : Going On Holiday – Part 2 18

القصة ٦ : شراء الطعام في الخارج ٢٠

Story 6 : Food Shopping Abroad 20

القصة ٧ : يوم مشغول في العطلات ٢٢

Story 7 : A Busy Day In The Holidays (1) 22

القصة ٨ : كعكة الشوكلاتة ٢٤

Story 8 : Chocolate Cake 24

القصة ٩ : كيف تخبز البسكويت ٢٧

Story 9 : How To Bake Scones 27

القصة ١٠ : الإنترنت ٣٠

Story 10 : Internet 30

القصة ١١ : نفق القناة ٣٢

Story 11 : Channel Tunnel 32

القصة ١٢ : النشرة الجوية ٣٥	
Story 12 : Weather Report 35	
القصة ١٣ : يوم مشغول في العطلات (٢) ٣٧	
Story 13 : A Busy Day In The Holidays (2) 37	
القصة ١٤ : الهواتف الذكية ٣٩	
Story 14 : Smartphones 39	
القصة ١٥ : شيستر ٤١	
Story 15 : Chester 41	
القصة ١٦ : عطلة عائلية – الجزء ١ .... ٤٣	
Story 16 : A Family Holiday – Part 1 43	
القصة ١٧ : عطلة عائلية – الجزء ٢ .... ٤٥	
Story 17 : A Family Holiday – Part 2 45	
القصة ١٨ : عطلة عائلية – الجزء ٣ .... ٤٧	
Story 18 : A Family Holiday – Part 3 47	
١٩ القص : عطلة عائلية_ الجزء ٤ .... ٤٩	
Story 19 : A Family Holiday – Part 4 49	
القصة ٢٠ : عطلة عائلية_ الجزء ٥ .... ٥١	
Story 20 : A Family Holiday – Part 5 51	
القصة ٢١ : الوصول للبيت ٥٣	
Story 21 : Getting Home 53	
القصة ٢٢ : الخروج للتسوق والغداء (١) ٥٦	
Story 22 : Out Shopping And For Lunch (1) 56	
القصة ٢٣ : الخروج للتسوق والغداء (٢) ٥٨	
Story 23 : Out Shopping And For Lunch (2) 58	
القصة ٢٤ : الخروج للتسوق والغداء (٣) ٦٠	
Story 24 : Out Shopping And For Lunch (3) 60	
القصة ٢٥ : نهاية العطلة (١) ٦٢	
Story 25 : End Of The Holidays (1) 62	
القصة ٢٦ : نهاية العطلة (٢) ٦٤	

Story 26 : End Of The Holidays (2) 64

القصة ٢٧ : نهاية العطلة (٣) ٦٨

Story 27 : End Of The Holidays (3) 68

القصة ٢٨ : نهاية العطلة (٤) ٧٠

Story 28 : End Of The Holidays (4) 70

القصة ٢٩ : نهاية العطلة (٥) ٧٢

Story 29 : End Of The Holidays (5) 72

القصة ٣٠ : نهاية العطلة (٦) ٧٤

Story 30 : End Of The Holidays (6) 74

Conclusion 76

Instructions On How To Download The Audio 77

About My Daily Arabic 79

مقدمة

INTRODUCTION

Everybody loves stories. I'm sure you do, too. So would you like to learn Arabic with the help of very short stories? It's fun and easy!

Most students who learn Arabic as a second language say they are having the most trouble with the following issues:

Lack of vocabulary

Difficulty in picking up grammar structures

Hesitation in speaking Arabic because of (1) pronunciation troubles or (2) listening comprehension problems.

This collection of 30 very short stories will help you solve those challenges. At only 300 words per story, this book is created for complete beginners with little or no previous experience in learning Arabic.

Learn new vocabulary

The stories in this book are written using the most useful Arabic words. After each story, you will find a list of vocabulary used in the story together with its English translation. There is no need to reach for a dictionary each time you encounter words you don't understand, and you will quickly learn new words as you go along.

Easily grasp Arabic sentence structures

Written with a good mix of descriptive sentences and simple dialogue, the stories will introduce you to different types of sentence structures. This way, you'll be able to naturally pick up Arabic grammar structures as you read the stories.

Practice your listening comprehension .

To be able to speak Arabic well, you need to expose your ears to a lot of spoken Arabic. You can do that by listening to the free audio narration of the stories. Listen to the words out loud and compare them to the written stories. Read along to the narration. Copy the correct pronunciation and practice the inflections. With enough practice, you will soon be able to get over your hesitations in speaking Arabic.

Learning Arabic as a second language can be a scary task. But with these short stories, you can make it as fun and as easy as possible. Before you know it, you have already learned hundreds of new Arabic words, exposed yourself to a variety of sentence structures, and listened to enough spoken Arabic that your pronunciation will improve greatly.

So go ahead. Start reading and have some fun!

Best of luck!

From My Daily Arabic

تريد نسخة غر يدوية؟

WANT THE HANDS-FREE VERSION?

If you would like a hands-free and purely auditory way to listen to Arabic Short Stories for Complete Beginners, check out the audio version in Audible. The audiobook provides you with almost 3 hours of stories, vocabulary, glossary---all of it and more--all in pure audio.

Listen to the stories while driving your car, enjoy it in your commute, while doing your chores or on your morning run. Anywhere you go and whatever you do, your Audible version of the book goes with you.

STORY 1 : FIRST DAY - PART 1

القصة ١ : اليوم الأول – الجزء ١

IMPORTANT: The link to download the MP3 is available at the end of this book (page 77)

المنبه مضبوط على ٠٠,٧. لكني استيقظت مبكرا. إنها ٣٠,٠٦ أنا متحمس ومتوتر في نفس الوقت

The alarm is set for 07.00 but I wake up early. It is 6.30. I am excited and nervous at the same time.

إنه الاثنين واليوم هو اليوم الذي ابدأ فيه وظيفتي الجديدة

It's Monday and today is the day I start my new job.

أنهض واستحم. ثم أتناول الإفطار. لست جائع لكني اشرب بعض القهوة وآكل موزة واحدة. اصنع شطيرة لغدائي

I get up and take a shower. Then I have breakfast. I am not hungry but drink some coffee and eat a banana. I make myself a sandwich for my lunch.

أذهب لكي ارتدي الملابس. اختار بدلة انيقة وبلوزة. انظر في المرآة. اعتقد أنني أبدو رسمية جدا وأغير رأيي. أجد فستان داكن اللون ومعطف ملائم واشعر براحة أكبر

I go to get dressed. I choose a smart suit and blouse. I look in the mirror. I think I look too formal and change my mind. I find a dark coloured dress and matching jacket and feel much more comfortable.

أنظف أسناني واضع بعض مساحيق التجميل

I clean my teeth and put on some make-up.

أجد مفاتيح سياراتي وأتفقد الوقت، وأدرك أني مبكرة جدا. انها ١٥,٠٧ وانا ابدأ العمل في ٣٠,٠٨

I find my car keys and then check the time, and realise that I am very early. It is 07.15 and I start work at 08.30!

أقرر أن ارحل على اى حال لأني لا اعلم كيف تكون حركة المرور في هذا الوقت. أقول وداعا الى بيتر وهنري.

I decide to leave anyway as I don't know what the traffic is like at this time. I say goodbye to Peter and Henry.

أصل في وقت جيد، على حوالي ٠٠,٠٨ اركن سيارتي في موقف السيارات، واشق طريقي إلى باب مكتبي الجديد. استغرق ذلك مني ٣ دقائق لأمشي إلى هناك

I arrive in good time, at about 08.00, park my car in the car park, and make my way to the door of my new office. It takes me 3 minutes to walk to there.

اطرق على الباب. رئيستي، جانيت، تأتي إلى الباب وتدخلني.

I knock on the door. My boss, Janet, comes to the door and lets me in.

بعض الأشخاص يعملون بالفعل وهي تقدمني إلى زملائي الجدد. هي تقول "هذه سارة. انها مديرة المكتب الجديدة"

Some people are already working and she introduces me to my new colleagues. She says, "This is Sarah. She's the new office manager".

الجميع لطفاء جدا ويقولون "أهلا"، "مرحبا" و"سررت بلقائك" عندما يتم تقديمي إليهم

Everybody is very friendly and they say "Hello", "Hi" and "Pleased to meet you," as I am introduced to them.

جانيت تريني أين الحمامات، والمطبخ، ثم تريني مكتبي. اجلس لكي ابدأ العمل.

Janet shows me where the toilets are, and the kitchen, then she shows me my desk. I sit down to start work.

لدى الكثير لأتعلمه والصباح يمر بسرعة جدا.

I have a lot to learn and the morning passes very quickly.

من قبل فترة طويلة، إنه وقت الغداء. لقد قررت أن اذهب إلى المطبخ لأكل شطيرتي وأصنع بعض القهوة.

Before long, it is lunchtime. I decide to go to the kitchen to eat my sandwich and make some coffee.

افتح حقيبتي وانظر بداخلها.

I open my bag and I look inside.

أفرغ حقيبتي. انظر الى كل شيء أفرغته منها. أين الشطيرة؟

I empty out my bag. I look at everything I have taken out. Where is the sandwich?

أنظر مجددا. لازال لا يوجد هناك شطيرة.

I look again. Still there is no sandwich.

فقط قهوة للغداء إذن

Just coffee for lunch then.

القصة الثانية : اليوم الأول – الجزء الثاني

STORY 2 : FIRST DAY - PART 2

IMPORTANT: The link to download the MP3 is available at the end of this book (page 77)

اجلس مع قهوتي في مطبخ الموظفين وانظر في رسائل هاتفي. العديد من الأصدقاء أرسلوا لي رسائل "حظ سعيد" ليومي الأول في وظيفتي الجديدة.

I sit with my coffee in the staff kitchen and look at my phone messages. Lots of friends are sending me "good luck" messages for my first day in my new job.

زملائي بدؤوا في القدوم إلى المطبخ فرادى وأزواجا وكلهم لطفاء ويقولون مرحبا. جاءوا إلى حيث اجلس وانضموا إلى بغدائهم.

My colleagues start to come into the kitchen in ones and twos and they are all friendly and say hello. They come over to where I am sitting and join me with their lunch.

سألوني أسئلة عن نفسي، أين اسكن، وإذا كنت في علاقة، وإذا كنت قد قمت بوظائف أخرى، وهكذا

They ask me questions about myself, where I live, if I'm in a relationship, what other jobs I have done, and so on.

إذا، ها هي الإجابات:

So, here are the answers:

اسمي سارة وأنا ٣٨ سنة.

My name is Sarah and I am 38 years old.

أعيش في سليمبردج وهي قرية صغير حوالي ٢٥ كيلومتر من المكتب. يوجد حوالي ١٥٠ بيت هناك، وحانة، ومكتب بريد ومكان لبيع الصحف، ومحل بقالة. الكنيسة في منتصف القرية ويوجد هناك منتزه بملاعب كرة قدم وملاعب تينيس حيث يذهب جميع الأطفال للعب.

I live in Slimbridge which is a small village about 25 kms away from the office. There are about 150 houses there, a pub, a post office and newsagent, and a grocery store. The church is at the centre of the village and there is a park with football pitches and tennis courts where all the children go to play.

أنا متزوجة من بيتر، مدرس، منذ ١١ عام ولدينا ابن، هنري، الذي يبلغ من العمر ٨ أعوام. هنري مليء بالطاقة ويريد أن يكون مشغولا. كلنا نحب أن نمارس الرياضة وهنري في فريق القرية لكرة القدم. هو يلعب المباريات في نهار السبت، وبيتر وأنا نذهب معه لكي نساعد عندما يمكننا.

I have been married to Peter, a teacher, for 11 years and we have a son, Henry, who is 8 years old. Henry is full of energy and wants to be busy. We all like to do sport and Henry is in the village football team. He plays matches on a Saturday morning, and Peter and I go along to help when we can.

زوجي وأنا نلعب الريشه الطائرة في أشهر الشتاء والتينس في الصيف. نذهب للسباحة مع هنري بقدر ما نستطيع.

My husband and I play badminton in the winter months and tennis during the summer. We go swimming with Henry as often as we can.

جميع وظائفي تضمن أعمال إدارية والعمل في مكتب. أنا جيدة في الأعمال الورقية ومنظمة جدا. عملت في بنك لمدة ٥ سنوات، في إدارة قسم، وتركت المكان عندما ولد هنري.

All of my jobs have involved administration and working in an office. I am good at paperwork and am very organised. I worked for a bank for five years, managing a department, and left there when Henry was born.

إذا الآن يعرفونني أفضل.

So now they know me better.

تنتهي استراحة الغداء وذهبا جميعا إلى المكتب نتحدث ونبتسم

The lunch break ends and we all go back to the office chatting and smiling.

القصة ٣ : اليوم الأول-الجزء الثالث

STORY 3 : FIRST DAY - PART 3

IMPORTANT: The link to download the MP3 is available at the end of this book (page 77)

يوم العمل ينتهي وأنا أفكر في رحلتي إلى المنزل. إنها ٣٠,١٧.

The working day comes to an end and I think about my journey home. It is 17.30.

أنا انتظر الجميع ليرحلوا ثم احمل حقيبتي واخذ مفاتيح المكتب. أنا مسئولة عن إغلاق المكتب، وفتحه في كل صباح، الآن أنا مدير المكتب. لذلك، احتاج أن أصل أولا في الصباح.

I wait for everybody to leave then pick up my bag and take out the office keys. I am responsible for locking the office, and opening it each morning, now that I am the office manager. So, I need to arrive first in the morning.

هناك جرس إنذار لضبطه ونوافذ للتحقق منها. ويجب أن أتأكد أن الحواسيب أغلقت. أنا افعل كل هذا ويستغرق الامر حوالي ١٥ دقيقة. أنا متأكدة أني سأكون أسرع غدا.

There is a security alarm to set as well as windows to check. And I must make sure the computers have been switched off. I do all of that and it takes me about 15 minutes. I'm sure I will be quicker tomorrow.

أقود مبتعدة في سيارتي وانضم إلى ازدحام مروري. إنها تستغرق مني أكثر من ساعة لقيادة ٢٥ كيلو متر إلى المنزل. أصل المنزل في ٤٥. ١٨.

I drive away in my car and join a traffic jam. It takes me more than an hour to drive the 25 kms home. I get home at 18.45.

قضيت وقت القيادة البطيئة في التفكير في السفر عن طريق القطار أو الحافلة بدلا من السيارة.

I spend the slow driving thinking about travelling by train or by bus instead of by car.

هذه خياراتي:

These are my options:

- محطة الحافلات تبعد حولي ٥ دقائق مشيا من منزلي والحافلات تنطلق مرة في كل ساعة. الرحلة تستغرق حوالي ساعة كاملة. عندما انزل في موقف الحافلة، أمامي ١٥ دقيقة من المشي. إذا أخذت الحافلة في الساعة ١٥,٠٧، سأرحل من المنزل في الساعة ١٠,٠٧، ٥ دقائق باكرا عن هذا الصباح. اعتقد أني سأصل المكتب في الساعة ٣٠,٠٨. هذا ضيق لأني ابدأ العمل في الساعة ٣٠,٠٨.
  - The bus stop is only 5 minutes' walk from my house and the buses run once per hour at a quarter past. The journey takes a full hour. When I get off at the bus station, I

have a 15-minute walk ahead of me. If I take the bus at 07.15, I will leave the house by 07.10, 5 minutes earlier than this morning. I think I will arrive at the office at 08.30. That's tight as I start work at 08.30.

- محطة القطار تبعد ١٠ دقائق قيادة من المنزل وهناك مساحة ضيقة لوقوف السيارات هناك. القطارات ترحل كل نصف ساعة، ٥ دقائق أو ٣٥ دقيقة بعد كل ساعة. الرحلة تستغرق ٢٥ دقيقة. المشي من المحطة إلى مكتبي حوالي ١٠ دقائق. لكي اخذ القطار، يجب أن اترك المنزل في ٠٧،٣٥ حتى أتمكن من ركن سيارتي، واذهب إلى رصيف القطار -القطار الذي سيتحرك في الساعة ٠٧،٣٥. اخرج من القطار في الساعة ٠٨،٠٠ ويمكن أن أكون موجودة في المكتب في الساعة ٠٨،١٠.

- The train station is a 10-minute drive from home and there is little parking there. The trains run every half hour at 5 and 35 minutes past each hour. The journey takes 25 minutes. The walk from the station to my office is 10 minutes. To take the train, I need to leave home at 07.15 – to be sure to be able to park, and to get to the platform – for the train at 07.35. I get off the train at 08.00 and can be at the office for 08.10.

عندما اعود إلى المنزل، أتفحص تكلفة التنقل بالحافلة والتنقل بالقطار. أقارن تكاليف التنقل بالسيارة – والدفع مقابل ركن السيارة وتكلفة الوقود.

When I get home, I check the cost of travelling by bus and travelling by train. I compare the costs with travelling by car - paying for the car park as well as the cost of the petrol.

بغض النظر عن التكلفة، أقرر أن الراحة أهم وأني سأستمر بالتنقل بالسيارة.

Regardless of the cost, I decide that convenience is more important and I will continue to travel by car.

القصة ٤ : الذهاب في عطلة – الجزء الأول

STORY 4 : GOING ON HOLIDAY – PART 1

IMPORTANT: The link to download the MP3 is available at the end of this book (page 77)

هناك الكثير لتفكر بشأنه عندما تخطط لقضاء عطلة.

There is a lot to think about when you are planning a holiday.

أولا، يجب عليك أن تقرر إلى أين تريد أن تذهب. هل لديك وجهة معينة فالاعتبار؟ ربما يكون لديك ولكن من الممكن الا يكون.

Firstly, you need to decide where to go. Do you have a destination in mind? You may have, but you may not.

قد تريد الذهاب في عطلة لممارسة الأنشطة، أو ربما عطلة لتتعلم عن ثقافة أو لغة مختلفة، أو ربما تريد الاستلقاء بجانب مسبح أو شاطئ وعدم فعلا اى شيء غير الاسترخاء لمدة العطلة. أو ربما مزيج من الثلاثة.

You may want to go on an activity holiday, or perhaps a holiday to learn about a different culture or language, or you may want to lie by a pool or on a beach and do nothing but relax for the duration of your holiday. Or perhaps a combination of all 3.

يجب عليك أن تقرر كيف تريد أن تقضي وقتك.

You have to decide on how you want to spend your time.

وأيضا ربما يجب عليك أن تقرر من تريد الذهاب معه، خاصة لو كنت أنت ورفقاء السفر لا يمكنكم الاتفاق على المكان الذي تريدون الذهاب إليه أو ماذا ستفعلون.

And you may also have to decide who to go with, especially if you and your travel party can't agree on where you're going or what you're doing.

في الواقع، خياراتك لا حصر لها، ولكن كذلك القرارات التي يتعين اتخاذها. الانترنت يمكنك من أن تأخذ في عين الاعتبار مدى واسع من الافكار، والوجهات والنشاطات، وان تكون أكثر مغامرة مما كنت عليه في اي وقت مضى.

In reality, your options are almost endless, but so are the decisions to be made. The Internet enables you to consider a vast range of ideas, destinations and activities, and to be more adventurous than it has ever been possible to be.

إذا ها هي الخطوات التي ينبغي اتخاذها:

So here are the steps to take:

STORY 4 : GOING ON HOLIDAY – PART 1 — القصة ٤ : الذهاب في عطلة – الجزء الأول

١. قرر من الذي ستذهب معه.

1. Decide who you are going to go away with.

٢. حدد ميزانيتك.

2. Agree your budget .

٣. حدد المواعيد التي يمكن فيها لكما (أو لكم) الذهاب.

3. Agree dates when you are both (or all) able to get away.

٤. ناقش كيف تريد أن تقضي وقتك – أن تكون مشغولا، أن تكون نشطا، أن تكون مثقفا، أن تكون كسولا، أو ان تكون شيئا آخر بالمرة. أو مزيج بين كل هذا. إذا لم تتمكن من الموافقة على كل شيء، ربما توافق على "أن تقوم بأمورك الخاصة" لبضع الوقت.

4. Discuss how you want to spend your time away – being busy, being active, being cultured, being lazy, or being something else altogether. Or a combination of them all. If you can't agree on everything, perhaps agree to 'do your own thing' for some of the time.

٥. اقضي بعض الوقت في التحدث عن المكان الذي تريد المكوث فيه: التخييم؟ في فندق أو فيلا؟ مع العائلة؟ تحت النجوم؟

5. Spend a little time talking about where you want to stay: camping? In a hotel or villa? With a family? Under the stars?

٦. فكر فيما إذا كنت ترغب أن تخطط العطلة بأكملها بنفسك، أو إذا كنت سترحب بمساعدة وكيل سفريات.

6. Consider if you want to plan the entire holiday yourselves, or whether you welcome the help of a travel agent.

٧. اختر البلد، ثم ضيق الأمر إلى وجهتك أو وجهاتك الفعلية، والنشاطات الرئيسية.

7. Agree your country, then narrow it down to your actual destination or destinations, and the key activities.

الآن بما أنك قد وصلت إلى هذا الحد، دعنا نفكر كيف يمكننا ان نجعل هذا يحدث.

Now that you've got this far, let's think about how we actually make this happen.

القصة ٥ : الذهاب في عطلة – الجزء الثاني

STORY 5 : GOING ON HOLIDAY – PART 2

IMPORTANT: The link to download the MP3 is available at the end of this book (page 77)

نحن نعرف أن هناك الكثير للتفكير فيه عندما تكون ذاهب في عطلة. قد يكون الأمر مرهق، لكنه ليس كذلك إذا كنت منظم جيدا.

We know there is a lot to think about when you're going on holiday. It can be stressful, but it isn't if you're well-organised.

الآن، أنت تعرف مع من انت ذاهب، ومتى. أنت تعرف كم هي المدة التي تريد أن تقضيها أو بامكانك ان تقضيها، أين تريد المكوث وماذا تريد أن تفعل حينما تكون هناك. أيضا أنت تعرف وجهتك، التي يمكن القول بانها أهم قرار عليك اتخاذه.

By now, you know who you're going with, and when. You know how much you want to spend or are able to spend, where you want to stay and what you want to do while you're away. You also know your destination, which is arguably the most important decision to be made.

لنفترض أنك ستنظم وتحجز بنفسك، بدون مساعدة وكيل سفريات. ستجد أن التكلفة اقل بهذه الطريقة، لكن المخاطرة أحيانا تكون أعلى، لذلك هو لن يكون قرارا سهلا.

Let's assume that you're arranging and booking this yourself, without the help of a travel agent. You will find the costs are lower this way, but the risks are sometimes higher, so it isn't be an easy decision.

النصائح والخطوات التالية ستجعل الأمور أكثر سهولة:

The following advice and steps will make things easier:

١. اختار شركة طيران جيدة لديك ثقة بها. تحقق من توفر رحلات في التاريخ الذي تريد السفر فيه.

1. Choose a good airline that you have confidence in. Check availability of flights for the dates you want to travel.

٢. ابحث عن أماكن للمكوث. تحقق من توفر أماكن للإقامة في التواريخ التي تريد الذهاب فيها. فكر فيما سيكون متضمنا وما سيكون اضافيا.

2. Look up places to stay. Check availability of accommodation for the dates you want to be away. Think about what is included and what is extra.

٣. تحقق من النشاطات التي تتوافق مع ما تريد ان تفعله حين تكون هناك.

3. Check out which activities match those you want to do while you are away.

٤. إذا تطابق كل شيء، تحقق من التواريخ مجددا، ثم احجز رحلات الطيران. ربما يكون لديك أكثر من مكان للإقامة لكن من المحتمل أن يكون هناك رحلة واحدة فقط تناسبك، لذلك احجز رحلاتك أولا.

4. If everything matches up, check your dates again, then book your flights. You probably have more than one place to stay but there is probably only one flight that suits you, so book your flights first.

٥. ثم تحقق من التواريخ مجددا، واحجز إقامتك.

5. Then check your dates again, and book your accommodation.

٦. والآن خطط لحجز نشاطاتك. وقبل أن تفعل، قرر ما هو الاهم بالنسبة لك. تفحص التأمين الذي يوفره كل مزود للانشطة وتأكد أنهم ياخذون سلامتك على محمل الجد.

6. And now plan to book your activities. Before you do, decide which are the most important to you. Look at the insurance each activity provider offers and make sure they take your safety seriously.

٧. الآن تحقق من التواريخ مجددا، ثم امضي قدما واحجز نشاطاتك.

7. Now, check your dates again, then go ahead and book your activities.

٨. وفي النهاية، خذ تأمين السفر على الفور. تأكد انه يغطي رحلاتك، والإقامة، والاحتياجات الطبية، وكل متعلقاتك. فكر في المال الذي تنفقه وتأكد أن كل شيء مغطى.

8. And finally, take out travel insurance straightaway. Make sure it covers you for your flights, accommodation, medical needs, and all your belongings. Think about how much you are spending and make sure everything is covered.

مع كل شيء، حافظ على إيصالاتك في مكان امن.

With everything, keep your receipts in a safe place.

والان، خطط فقط أن تستمتع برحلتك، متى خطر على بالك.

And now, just plan to enjoy your trip, whenever it comes around.

القصة ٦ : شراء الطعام في الخارج

STORY 6 : FOOD SHOPPING ABROAD

IMPORTANT: The link to download the MP3 is available at the end of this book (page 77)

شراء الطعام في بلد أجنبي هو متعة وتجربة للتعلم. يمكن من فهم العديد من الاختلافات الثقافية وربما فهم أسلوب آخر في الحياة.

Shopping for food in a foreign country is a pleasure and a learning experience. It enables you to see and understand so many cultural differences and, perhaps, to understand the different way of life.

في البلاد الباردة، الطعام غالبا ما يكون ثقيل وملئ بالكاربوهيدرات، لأن الناس الذين يعيشون هناك يحتاجون إلى حرق المزيد من السعرات للمحافظة على حرارتهم. هم يختاروا الأطعمة التي ستملئ معدتهم وتدفئهم من الداخل، وقد تستغرق الكثير من الوقت لطبخها. هم يستمتعون عندما يكون الفرن يعمل، أو النار مشتعله لعدة ساعات إذا لزم الامر، لطبخ طعامهم بعناية. إنها مصدر إضافي للحرارة في المناخ البارد. أحيانا يبدو ان المتاجر تحتوي فقط على الأطعمة التي تبدوا مملة. لديها القليل من الألوان حيث أنها تنمو تحت الأرض أو في الظلام، وترى القليل من الشمس. لذلك قد تبدوا غير مثيرة للشهية أو للاهتمام. إنها بالتأكيد تبدوا اقل إغراء لأكلها، لكنها ستظل لذيذة.

In cold countries, food is often heavy and full of carbohydrates, as the people who live there need to burn extra calories to keep themselves warm. They choose foods that will fill their stomachs and warm them from the inside, and which may take a long time to cook. They are happy to have an oven on, or a fire burning, for hours if necessary, to cook their food thoroughly. It is an additional source of heat in a cold climate. Often, the supermarkets only contain food which looks a little boring. It has little colour as it's grown underground or in the dark, and sees little sun. It can therefore seem unappetising or uninteresting. It certainly looks less tempting to eat, but will still be tasty.

في البلاد الأكثر دفئا، في المقابل، الناس غالبا لا يفضلون طهي الطعام كثيرا على الإطلاق. هم لا يريدون حرارة فرن أو نار لجعل منازلهم أكثر سخونة، وهم لا يريدون وضع طعام ساخن في اجسادهم. ربما يختاروا أطعمة بسيطة يمكن أكلها نية، لذلك الخضروات الطازجة والفاكهة، والسلطة، غالبا ما ترى، بالإضافة إلى الأطعمة التي إذا تم طبخها، فإنها تستغرق القليل من الوقت في الطهي.

In warmer countries, on the other hand, people often prefer not to cook very much at all. They do not want the heat from an oven or fire to make their home even warmer, and they do not want to put hot food inside their body. They may choose simple food that is best eaten raw, so fresh fruit and vegetables, and salads, are often what is seen, as well as foods that, if cooked, take little time to cook through.

في البقالات والمتاجر الكبيرة في البلاد الدافئة، سترى مجموعة من الفاكهة والخضروات الملونة لاغرائك، بالإضافة

إلى مدى واسع من الأعشاب. الشمس تجلب الألوان للأطعمة المتوفرة. سيكون هناك عادة أطعمة لم ترها أو تسمع بها من قبل. يمكنك رؤيتها بجانب تشكيلة من الأسماك، البعض منها قد يكون موجود فقط في المياه المحلية.

In the markets and supermarkets in a warm country, you will see an array of colourful fruit and vegetables to tempt your palette, as well as a big range of herbs. The sun brings colour to the foods available. There will often be foods you have never seen or heard of before. These will very often be seen alongside a variety of fish, some of which are only found in the local waters.

عندما تسافر، ابذل مجهود لكي تأكل وتستمتع بالأطعمة المحلية ولكي تعانق الثقافة التي تجربها.

When you travel, make an effort to eat and enjoy the local foods and to embrace the culture you are experiencing.

STORY 7 : A BUSY DAY IN THE HOLIDAYS (1)

القصة ٧ : يوم مشغول في العطلات

IMPORTANT: The link to download the MP3 is available at the end of this book (page 77)

"أبي! أبي! هل يمكننا الذهاب إلى السباحة؟"

"Dad! Dad! Can we go swimming?".

"إنه وقت النوم الآن. يمكننا التحدث في هذا الأمر صباحا"

"It's time for bed now. We can talk about it in the morning."

إنها العطلة المدرسية وأنا كمدرس اعتني بابننا هنري. والكلب شارلي. هنري يبلغ من العمر ٨ سنوات و ملئ بالطاقة، وهو يريد أن يبقى مشغولا. هو يريد الخروج وفعل شيء ما كل يوم لكن يجب علينا القيام ببعض المهام في المنزل كذلك.

It's the school holidays and, as I am teacher, I look after our son, Henry. And the dog, Charlie. Henry is 8 years old and full of energy, and wants to be busy. He wants to go out and do something every day but we need to do some jobs at home as well.

هو يقوم مبكرا كل صباح واليوم ليس مختلف. هو يسأل على الفور إذا كان بإمكاننا الذهاب للسباحة. أنا اعرض عليه صفقة.

He gets up early every day and today is no different. He asks immediately if we can go swimming. I offer him a deal.

"يمكننا الذهاب للسباحة عندما ننتهي من بعض المهام. هل ستساعدني في القيام بهذه المهام؟"

"We can go swimming when we have finished some jobs. Will you help me to do the jobs?"

ينظر إلى، وهو لايزال غير متأكد ومتوترا مما قد يجب عليه فعله. هو لا يجيب لذلك أنا أوضح:

He looks at me, still unsure, nervous about what he might have to do. He doesn't answer so I explain:

"يجب علينا إفراغ غسالة الصحون، ونغسل، ونضع الغسيل. ونكنس. أيهم تريد فعله؟" سألته.

"We have to empty the dishwasher, wash up, put the washing on, and hoover. Which do you want to do?", I ask him.

ينظر إلي مرة اخرى, مازال غير متأكد.

He looks at me again, still unsure.

وفي النهاية يقول "هل يمكنني غسل السيارة عوضا عن ذلك؟".

Eventually he says, "Can I wash the car instead?".

أفكر بحذر فيما يعرضه. السيارة تحتاج إلى التنظيف لكني لا أريد الاستسلام بسهولة. أنا أريده أن يفهم أن هناك عمل جاد لفعله ويجب ان يكتسب هديته.

I think carefully about what he is offering. The car does need cleaning but I don't want to give in too easily. I want him to understand that there is hard work to do and he has to earn his treats.

أتذكر انه غسل سيارتي مرة واحدة من قبل، لكنني كنت معه. هذه المرة يجب عليه أن يفعلها بمفرده.

I remember that he washed my car once before, but I was with him. This time he needs to do it on his own.

أتوقف وأتجول في أنحاء المطبخ، أفكر. يسألني مرارا وتكرارا، "أرجوك أبي، هل يمكنني غسل السيارة عوضا عن ذلك؟".

I pause and wander around the kitchen, thinking. He asís me ovar and ovar, "Please Dad, can I wash the car instead?".

بعد مهلة معقولة، استسلم. اخذه إلى المرأب لأجد الدلو والاسفنجة وشامبو السيارة، واتركه يقم بذلك.

After a reasonable pause, I give in. I take him to the garage to find the bucket, sponge and car shampoo, and leave him to it.

استمر في مهامي في المنزل في سلام واستمع للإذاعة، واطمئن عليه كل ١٥ دقيقة. أنا أرى انه يعمل بجد ويأخذ عمله بجديه.

I carry on with my jobs in the house, in peace and listening to the radio, and I check on him every 15 minutes. I see he is working hard and taking his job seriously.

هو ينتهي ويقوم برمي الإسفنجة في الدلو ويصرخ، "أبي لقد انتهيت"، أذهب خارجا للتحقق من عمله.

He finishes and throws the sponge into the bucket with a shout of, "Dad, I've finished," and I go outside to check his work.

أنا منبهر بمدى نظافة ولمعان سيارتي وأقول له انه منظف سيارات مبهر.

I am amazed at how clean and shiny my car is and tell him he is an amazing car cleaner.

نعود الى داخل المنزل ونحزم ملابس السباحة، ونتجه إلى حمام السباحة.

We go back into the house and pack our swimming clothes, and head to the swimming pool.

بعد سباحتنا، يقول لي، "أنا استمتعت بهذا جدا، أبي. أنا اشعر أنني استحق هديتي!".

After our swim, he says, "I really enjoyed that, Dad. I really feel as if I earned my treat!".

وأنا اتفق معه.

And I agree with him.

القصة ٨ : كعكة الشوكلاتة

STORY 8 : CHOCOLATE CAKE

IMPORTANT: The link to download the MP3 is available at the end of this book (page 77)

عندما تخبز الكعك تذكر التالي:

When baking cakes, remember the following:

يفضل أن يؤكل الكعك ساخنا.

الأطباق الساخنة يمكنها أن تحرقك إذا لمستهم.

يجب عليك أن تقيس المكونات بحذر.

إنه من الأفضل الاستمتاع بهم وهم طازجين.

Cakes are better eaten warm.

Hot dishes can burn you if you touch them.

You must measure the ingredients carefully.

It is better to enjoy them while they are fresh.

لنفكر ببعض التفاصيل الهامة عند صنع كعكة شوكلاتة.

Let's think about some important details when making a chocolate cake.

- المكونات:
- ١٠٠ جرام من الدقيق
- ١٠٠ جرام من السكر
- ١٠٠ جرام من الزبدة
- بيضتان
- شوكولاتة – حقيقية أو مسحوق

INGREDIENTS:

- 100 grams of flour
- 100 grams of sugar
- 100 grams of butter

- 2 eggs
- Chocolate – real chocolate or powdered

إذا اتبعت التعليمات بحذر، ستكون لذيذة.

If you follow the instructions carefully, it will be delicious.

١. اشتري كل المكونات مسبقا واستخدمهم وهم طازجين.

1. Buy all of the ingredients in advance and use them while they are still fresh.

٢. قس المكونات الأساسية – البيض، الدقيق، الزبد والسكر – بكل حذر ثم اخلطهم معا حتى يصبح المزيج ناعم ودهني. هذا ربما يستغرق ٥-١٠ دقائق. انها أسهل إذا كانت الزبدة لينه بالفعل.

2. Measure out the main ingredients - eggs, flour, butter and sugar - very carefully and then mix them together until the mixture is smooth and creamy. This may take 5 to 10 minutes. It is easier if the butter is already soft.

٣. أضف الشوكلاتة الذائبة عندما يبرد المزيج في الثلاجة لمدة ١٠دقائق. إذا أضفت شوكلاتة حقيقية، أذبها بهدوء وبطء. إذا أفرطت في تسخين الشوكلاتة، ستصبح متكتلة ولن يمكنك استخدامها. إذا كنت تفضل إضافة مسحوق الشوكلاتة بدل من الشوكلاتة الذائبة، تأكد إنها منخولة أولا ثم أضفها ببطء لمزيج الكعكة.

3. Add the melted chocolate when the mixture has cooled in the fridge for 10 minutes. If you add real chocolate, melt it very gently and slowly. If you overheat the chocolate, it will go lumpy and you will not be able to use it. If you prefer to add powdered chocolate instead of melted chocolate, make sure it is sieved first and then add it slowly to the cake mixture.

٤. أشعل الفرن حتى يصبح ساخنا بدرجة كافية عندما تكون مستعد لوضع المزيج لكي يُطبخ، وحتى تطبخ الكعكة بشكل متساوي.

4. Turn on the oven so that it is warm enough when you are ready to put the mixture in to cook, and so that the cake is cooked evenly.

٥. قم بصب المزيج في طبق مدهون بالزيت (أو طبقين).

5. Pour the mixture into a greased dish (or 2 dishes).

٦. عندما تكون الأطباق جاهزة، ضعهم في الفرن. اطبخ لمدة ٢٠ دقيقة.

6. When the dishes are ready, put them in the oven. Cook for 20 minutes.

٧. عندما تكون الكعكة جاهزة، تأكده من عدم لمس طبق الخبز بيديك عندما تخرجه من الفرن لأنه سيكون ساخن جدا. استخدم قفازا للفرن.

7. When the cake is ready, remember not to touch the baking dish with your hands when you take it out of the oven as it will be too hot. Use an oven glove.

٨. اخرج الكعكة من علبتها واتركها لكي تبرد.

8. Turn the cake out of its tin and leave to cool.

٩. بمجرد أن تبرد، اقطع قطعة واستمتع.

9. Once cool, cut a slice and enjoy.

STORY 9 : HOW TO BAKE SCONES

القصة ٩ : كيف تخبز البسكويت

البسكويت من حلوى وقت الشاي الانجليزي الكلاسيكية، وهو سهل جدا في صنعه. وصفة البسكويت هذه سهلة أيضا في تغييرها إذا أردت تجربة طعم آخر أو حشو.

Scones are a classic English tea-time treat, and are very easy to make. This scone recipe is also easy to change if you want to try a different flavour or filling.

- المكونات
- ٢٢٥ جرام من الدقيق ذاتي التخمير
- القليل من الملح
- ٥٥ جرام من الزبدة اللينة
- ٢٥ جرام من السكر الناعم
- ١٥٠ مل من اللبن
- بيضة مخفوقة (يمكنك استخدام القليل من اللبن كبديل)

- INGREDIENTS:
- 225g of self-raising flour
- a pinch of salt
- 55g of soft butter
- 25g of caster sugar
- 150ml of milk
- 1 free-range egg, beaten, to glaze (although you could, alternatively, use a little milk).

الطريقة:

METHOD:

١. سخن الفرن إلى درجة حرارة ٢٠٠ مئوية

1. Heat the oven to 200°C.

٢. ادهن ورقة الخبز، أو ضع قطعة من الورق المقاوم للدهون فوقها.

2. Lightly grease a baking sheet, or put a piece of greaseproof paper on it.

٣. اخلط الدقيق والملح معا، ثم افرك الزبد اللينة.

3. Mix together the flour and salt, then rub in the softened butter.

٤. ضع السكر، القليل في كل مرة، ثم أضف اللبن لصنع عجينة طرية.

4. Stir in the sugar, a little at a time, and then add the milk to make a soft dough.

٥. اعجن المزيج بيديك في وعاء للخلط، ثم اقلبه على سطح مغطى بالدقيق ثم اعجنه مجددا برفق.

5. Work the mixture well with your hands in the mixing bowl, then turn it out onto a floured surface and knead it again lightly.

٦. ساوي المزيج في شكل دائري في سمك حوالي ٢ سم. استخدم قاطعة سمكها ٥ سم لصنع بسكويت دائري، وضعهم على ورقة الخبز.

6. Pat out the mixture into a round shape roughly 2cm thick. Use a 5cm cutter to make rounds / individual scones, and place them on the baking sheet.

٧. اجمع ما تبقى من العجين وكرر الخطوة ٦. استمر في فعل هذا حتى تكون استخدمت المزيج كله لصنع البسكويت.

7. Pull together what is left of the dough and repeat Step 6. Keep doing this until you have used all of the mixture to make scones.

٨. ادهن أعلى البسكويت ببيض مخفوق (أو لبن). ضع ورقة الخبز في الفرن.

8. Brush the tops of the scones with the beaten egg (or the milk). Put the baking sheet in the oven.

٩. اخبز لحوالي ١٢-١٥ دقيقة حتى يرتفع ويصبح ذهبي من أعلى.

9. Bake for between 12 and 15 minutes until well risen and golden on the top.

برده على رف السلك ويقدم مع الزبدة ومربى جيدة (مربى الفراولة تعمل بشكل جيد)، أو ربما بعض القشطة بدل من الزبدة.

Cool on a wire rack and serve with butter and a good jam (strawberry works very well), or maybe some clotted cream instead of the butter.

يمكنك تغيير الوصفة بإضافة الفاكهة المجففة في الخطوة ٤. يمكنك أيضا إضافة بعض التوابل مثل جوزة الطيب أو القرفة.

You can change the recipe by adding dried fruit at Step 4. You can also add some spices such as nutmeg or cinnamon.

يمكنك صنع بسكويت بالجبن (مملح) عن طريق عدم إضافة السكر وإضافة ١٠٠ جرام من الجبن المبشورة. جبن قوية مثل الشيدر تعمل بشكل أفضل.

You can make cheese (savoury) scones by leaving out the sugar and adding 100 grams of grated cheese. A strong cheese such as cheddar works best.

أستمتع!

Enjoy!

القصة ١٠ : الإنترنت

STORY 10 : INTERNET

مع قدوم التكنولوجيا الحديثة، الناس يمكنهم الاستمتاع اليوم بحياة ملائمة ومريحة مقارنة بالأجيال الأقدم.

With the advent of modern technology, people today can enjoy more convenient and comfortable lives compared to the older generations.

في عصر المعلومات هذا، محركات البحث مثل جوجل، وسفاري، وبينج هي من ضمن البرامج الحاسوبية الأكثر استخداماً بسبب ملائمتهم وإمكانياتهم.

In this Information Age, search engines such as Google, Safari and Bing are amongst the most widely used computer applications because of their convenience and potential.

بمهارات الحاسوب الأساسية، يمكن للناس بسهولة إيجاد حلول لكل مشاكلهم وفي نفس الوقت إرضاء فضولهم.

With only basic computer skills, people can easily find answers to their problems at the same time as satisfying their curiosity.

الكثير من الطلاب يستخدمون محركات البحث بطريقة مفرطة لأسباب أكاديمية. هم يعتمدوا أحيانا على محركات البحث فقط في معلوماتهم ولا يستكشفوا مصادر المعلومات الأخرى، مثل قراءة الكتب أوالمشاركة في محادثة مع زملائهم الطلاب. يمكنهم بسهول فقدان إحساسهم بالفضول.

Many students make excessive use of search engines for academic purposes. They sometimes rely solely on search engines for their information and do not explore other sources of information, such as reading books or engaging in conversations with their fellow students. They can easily lose their sense of curiosity.

الطلاب الأذكياء يقضوا وقت أكثر في جمع المعلومات من العالم الحقيقي بدلا من المصادر العامة عبر الانترنت ولذلك يتوصلوا إلى أجوبة أكثر تميز وفردية وإثارة للاهتمام.

Wise students spend more time gathering their information from the real world rather than public, online sources and so come up with more unique, individual, and interesting answers.

الحواسيب والتكنولوجيا تلعب دورا هاما في حياة الناس، لكن يمكن أيضا أن تؤثر على خصوصيتهم

Computers and technology do play a vital role in peoples' lives, but they can also affect their privacy.

إنه من السهل للمجرمين أن يروا بيانات الشخص، وهذه المخاطرة تزين إذا كان الأشخاص لا يفكرون جديا في الطريقة التي يستخدمون بها الحاسوب.

It is easy for criminals to see an individual's information and the risk of this is greater if an individuals do not think seriously about how they use their computer.

انتهاك الخصوصية ربما يبدوا محتم في هذا العصر الرقمي، لكنه لا ينبغي أن يكون. لقد كان من المستحيل تقريبا الحصول على البيانات البنكية الخاصة بشخص معين، تاريخ الميلاد، رقم الضمان الاجتماعي، بدون إذن منه. لكن اليوم، كل هذه المعلومات تبدوا سهلة الاكتشاف.

Invasion of privacy may seem inevitable in this digital age, but it should not be. It used to be almost impossible to find out somebody's bank details, date of birth, or social security number, without their permission. But today, these details seem to be so easy to find out.

مواقع التواصل الاجتماعي تشجع الناس على أن يكونوا منفتحين حيال حياتهم الشخصية وان يشاركوا معلومات قد تكون مجدية للذين يريدون أن يستخدموها لأغراض إجرامية او خبيثة. الناس بطبيعة الحال اجتماعيون ويريدون مشاركة تجاربهم، لكن فعل هذا عن طريق استخدام التكنولوجيا يمكن أن يسبب مشاكل في حياتهم.

Social networking sites encourage people to be open about their private lives and to share information that is useful to others who wish to use it for criminal or malicious purposes. People are naturally sociable and want to share their experiences, but doing so through the use of technology can cause them problems in their lives.

يمكن للأفراد أن يتحكموا في حياتهم وكيفية استخدامهم للحاسوب والانترنت هي جزء مهم من ذلك.

Individuals can take control of their lives and how they use their computer and the Internet is a significant part of this.

القصة ١١ : نفق القناة

STORY 11 : CHANNEL TUNNEL

إذا كنت تريد التنقل بالسيارة بين بريطانيا وأوروبا، التنقل عن طريق نفق القناة هي أسهل طريقة لتفعل ذلك.

If you want to travel by car between Britain and Europe, travelling through the Channel Tunnel is the easy way to do it.

التوجه لهناك عن طريق الطريق السريع بسيط وهو معلم جيدا.

Getting there on the motorway is very straightforward and it is well-signposted.

حالما تصل، ستكون عملية بسيطة وعادة ما تتم بسلاسة.

Once you arrive, it is a simple process and it usually goes smoothly.

إذا كنت حجزت مسبقا، يمكنك استخدام تحصيل الرسوم التلقائي. ببساطة ادخل رقم الحجز المرجعي. سترى إذا كان قطارك في الموعد، وإذا لم يكن كذلك، في اى وقت يمكنك أن تغادر. عن طريق الحجز المسبق النفق الأوروبي يفعل كل ما يمكنه فعلا لتأمين تنقلك على القطار الذي قمت بحجزه. انت تُنصح بأن تصل ٤٥ دقيقة مبكرا عن موعد المغادرة المحجوز مسبقا، على الرغم من ذلك اسمح بالكثير من الوقت أثناء شهور الصيف المزدحمة.

If you have pre-booked, you can use an automatic toll booth. You simply enter your booking reference number. You will see if your train is running on time and, if not, what time you can depart. With pre-booking, Eurotunnel does all that it can to ensure you travel on the train you have booked. You are advised to arrive 45 minutes ahead of your pre-booked departure time, although allow plenty of time during the busy summer months.

إذا لم تكن قد حجزت مسبقاً، يمكنك أن تدفع عندما تصل. عن طريق هذا الخيار، ستسافر على القطار التالي الذي يوجد به مكان.

If you have not pre-booked, you can pay when you arrive. With this option, you travel on the next train that has a space.

بكلتا الحالتين، سيتم إعطائك رمز لتعليقه في سيارتك. تذكر الرمز الخاص بك!

Either way, you will be given a letter code to hang in your car. Remember your code!

بعد تحصيل الرسوم، انت تذهب من خلال الصالة. إنه من النافع دائما أن تذهب إلى الحمام وتتفقد المتاجر لأشياء اللحظة الأخيرة التي ربما قد تكون نسيتها. هناك مجموعة من المتاجر التي تعرض العطور، الأشياء الكهربية، الكحول والحلوى، أيضا عدد من الاماكن لتناول الطعام.

After the toll booth, you go through to the terminal. It's always useful to visit the toilet and to check the shops for any last-minute items you have forgotten. There is a range of shops offering perfume, electrical items, alcohol and sweets, as well as a number of places to eat.

أنظر في الشاشات لكي تعرف اى قطار يحمل الآن وأى رموز تتعلق بهذا القطار، سيعلمونك أيضا متى سيكون من المرجح أن يُنادى رمزك. هذا يساعدك في معرفة إذا كان لديك وقت لشرب القهوة أو شيء أكثر.

Look at the screens to find out which train is loading currently and which letter code relates to that train. They also let you know when your letter is likely to be called. This helps you to know if you have time for a coffee or something more.

عندما يُنادى رمزك، ارجع إلى سيارتك وتتبع العلامات. ستذهب خلال إدارة الجوازات ثم منطقة الأمن، قبل أن تنضم إلى الطابور للقيادة إلى القطار.

When your letter is called, return to your car and follow the signs. You will go through passport control and then through a security area, before joining the queue to drive on to the train.

هذه الطوابير يتم إداراتها عن كثب ويجب عليك تحسن التصرف وتنتظر في الخط.

These queues are closely managed and you must behave yourself and wait in line.

عندما يتم مناداتك إلى القطار، قد بحذر وادخل القطار ببطء لأنه صغير وضيق من الداخل. استمر حتى يخبرك أحد من الموظفين أن توقف السيارة.

When you are called to board the train, drive carefully and enter the train slowly as it is quite small and narrow inside. Proceed until a member of staff tells you to park.

عندما توقف السيارة، يجب عليك الاستماع بحرص للمعلومات الأمنية التي تسمعها. إنه من الهام جدا ان تتبع التعليمات – لسلامتك وسلامة المسافرين. على سبيل المثال، التصوير بالأنوار الخاطفة ممنوع.

When you park, you must listen carefully to the security information you hear. It is very important that you follow the instructions – for your own safety and that of the other travellers. For example, flash photography is not allowed.

أنت تُنصح بأن تنتظر في سيارتك أثناء العبور، ويجب أن تترك شباك السيارة مفتوح.

You are advised to wait by your car during the crossing, and must leave a car window open.

هناك فحوصات أمنية على السيارة ومن ثم ستسمع المحرك يستعد لبدأ الرحلة. الرحلة نفسها تستمر فقط ٣٥ دقيقة، والوقت يمر سريعا.

There are security checks on the vehicle and then you will hear the engines getting ready to start the journey. The journey itself lasts only 35 minutes, and the time flies by.

بعض السائقين يستغلون هذا الوقت لكي يناموا قبل الاستمرار في رحلتهم. البعض الأخر يستخدموا هذا الوقت في أكل وجبة خفيفة أو لعب الألعاب.

Some drivers use this time to sleep before continuing their onward journey. Others use the time to eat a snack or to play games.

عندما تصل إلى الجانب الأخر، سيكون هناك فحوصات أمنية كثيرة قبل أن يفتحوا الباب ويمكنك القيادة بعيدا.

When you reach the other side, there are more security checks before they open the doors and you drive away.

التنقل عبر نفق القناة سهل جدا.

Travelling through the Channel Tunnel is so easy.

القصة ١٢ : النشرة الجوية

STORY 12 : WEATHER REPORT

ها هي النشرة الجوية للبلد في ١٢ ساعة القادمة.

Here is the country's forecast for the next 12 hours.

اليوم في شمال البلاد، الجو بارد ورطب. الأمطار الشديدة متوقعة، بنسبة هطول ١٠ سم بين منتصف اليوم والساعة ١٦,٠٠، وأيضا هناك احتمال أن تمطر ثلجا. الحرارة منخفضة في هذا الوقت من السنة، ومع حلول الليل، هناك خطر الصقيع. كن أكثر حذرا إذا كنت تقود، واحترس من الجليد على الطرق.

In the north of the country today, it is cold and wet. Heavy rain is forecast, with up to 10cm falling between midday and 16.00, and there is also a risk of sleet and hail. The temperature is low for the time of year and, as night falls, there is a risk of frost. Take extra care if you are driving, and look out for ice on the roads.

غرب البلاد يبدو معتدلا صباحا، لكن هناك احتمالية عالية لسقوط الامطار خاصة في فترة ما بعد الظهيرة. كن مستعدا لبعض العواصف إذا أمطرت، مع رياح قوية، وعاصفة قوية، وبرق ورعد. خذ معك مظلة لكن تذكر ألا تستخدمها إذا سمعت الرعد أو رأيت البرق، وابق على الحيوانات الاليفة داخل المنزل! المساء جاف لكنه لايزال عاصفا، مع ارتفاع في درجات الحرارة حتى تصبح طبيعية لهذا الوقت من السنة.

The west of the country is looking fair in the morning, but there is still a high risk of rain, especially in the afternoon. Be prepared for some storms if it rains, with strong winds, some gale force, and thunder and lightning. Take an umbrella but remember not to use it if you hear thunder or see lightning, and keep your pets indoors! The evening is dry but still windy, with temperatures rising so that they are normal for the time of year.

شرق البلاد متوقع أن يكون ضبابيا، خاصة في الصباح، يبدو انه رطب وبارد، لكن هذا ليس نتيجة للمطر على الإطلاق. احترس من الرياح القوية، والعواصف، الاتيه من الغرب. درجات الحرارة طبيعية بالنسبة لهذا الوقت من السنة والعواصف في الغرب ستنتهي قبل أن تصل إلى الشرق.

The east of the country is expected to be foggy or misty, especially in the morning. It feels damp, and therefore cool, but it is not due to rain at all. Beware of strong winds, some gale force, coming from the west. The temperatures are normal for the time of year and the storms in the west will die out before reaching the east.

جنوب البلاد يستمتع بجو جميل. هناك نسيم خفيف ودرجات حرارة دافئة، ولا احتمال للأمطار. سقوط الأمطار في الجنوب يستمر منخفضا لهذا الوقت من السنة، مع درجات حرارة مرتفعة في هذا الوقت من السنة. بسبب درجات الحرارة المرتفعة، تأكد من أن تأخذ الماء معك عندما تذهب خارجا. تأكد من أن الحيوانات الأليفة والأطفال ليسوا في خطر التعرض لحروق شمسية أو الجفاف.

The south of the country is enjoying fine weather. There is a light breeze and warm temperatures, with no risk of rain. Rainfall in the south continues to be low for the time of year, with the temperatures high for the time of year. Because of the high temperatures, make sure you take water with you when you go out. Make sure your pets and children are not at risk of getting sunburn or dehydrated.

النشرة الجوية للغد تبدوا معتدلة وجافة.

The forecast for tomorrow looks fine and dry.

STORY 13 : A BUSY DAY IN THE HOLIDAYS (2)

(القصة ١٣ : يوم مشغول في العطلات(٢

أنا وهنري نتحدث عن كيف أن العمل ـ والقيام بالوظائف ـ يساعدك في الحصول على الهدايا، أو ربما، المال. هو يتذكر تنظيف السيارة والذهاب للسباحة كمكافأة له.

Henry and I talk about how working - and doing jobs - helps you to earn treats or, perhaps, money. He remembers cleaning the car and being taken swimming as his reward.

يستيقظ ـ مليئا بالطاقة ويريد أن يكون مشغول، كالعادة ـ ويسأل عن المهام التي يمكنه ان يفعلها اليوم.

He gets up – full of energy and wanting to be busy, as always – and asks what jobs he can do today.

بعد الإفطار، نبدأ بالتفكير فيما يمكنه فعله حقا، بالنظر إلى حجمه. ثم نتكلم عما يجب فعله اليوم.

After breakfast, we start by thinking about what he can actually do, given his size. Then we talk about what needs to be done today.

أنا أقول أننا نحتاج لبعض اللبن والخبز من البقالة فالقرية. هنري يقول أنّ الحشيش يحتاج القص ويجب تمشية الكلب. أنا أشير إلى أن الحمام يحتاج إلى التنظيف وان المنزل يحتاج ان يكنس.

I say we need some milk and bread from the grocery store in the village. Henry says the lawn needs mowing and we must walk the dog. I mention that the bathroom needs a good clean and the house needs to be hoovered.

نتفق على أن هنري يمكنه تمشية الكلب إلى البقالة، يربطه في الخارج، ثم يدخل لشراء اللبن والخبز. هو ينطلق مع كلب متحمس ويقفز في مشيته. أنا أجد قفازات مطاطية وأدوات تنظيف، وانطلق إلى تنظيف الحمام. هذه اقل مهمة أحبها، لكن لا يمكنني أن أطلب من هنري فعلها. عندما انتهي، ثم اخذ المكنسة من الدولاب واكنس المنزل. كل مكان يبدوا أكثر نظافة عندما انتهي.

We agree that Henry can walk the dog to the grocery store, tie him up outside, then go in and buy the milk and the bread. He sets off with an excited dog and a spring in his step. I find the rubber gloves and cleaning products, and set to cleaning the bathroom. This is the job I like the least, but I can't ask Henry to do it. When I finish, I then take the hoover from the cupboard and hoover around the house. Everywhere looks and feels much cleaner when I finish.

هنري يعود إلى المنزل باللبن والخبز والكلب، وقالب من الشوكلاتة لكل منا لكي نتناوله لاحقا. فكرة عظيمة!

Henry comes home with the milk and the bread, and the dog, and a bar of chocolate for each of us to have later. Great idea!

نقرر أننا سنجز العشب معا. إنه يستغرق بعض الوقت. أنا ادفع جزازة العشب وهنري يحصد العشب المقطوع. هو

يضعه في كومة في الركن، بعيدا عن الطريق.

We decide to mow the lawn together. It takes a while. I push the mower and Henry rakes up the grass cuttings. He puts them in a pile in the corner, out of the way.

إنه يكاد يكون وقت الغداء ونحن على وشك الانتهاء من مهماتنا. هنري ينظم الطاولة وأنا اعد لنا شطيرة. نجلس لكي نأكل الغداء معا.

It's almost lunch time and we have almost finished our jobs. Henry sets the table and I make us a sandwich. We sit down to eat lunch together.

نحاول أن نقرر ما الذي سنفعله بعد الظهيرة ونتفق أن كلانا مرهق جدا ونريد المكوث في المنزل والاسترخاء، ونعجب بعملنا. ونأكل الشوكلاتة بالطبع.

We try to decide what to do in the afternoon and agree that we are both too tired and just want to stay at home and relax, and admire our work. And eat our chocolate, of course.

فكرة أخرى عظيمة!

Another great idea!

القصة ١٤ : الهواتف الذكية

STORY 14 : SMARTPHONES

لقد مر ما يزيد عن العقد منذ أن اخترعت الهواتف الذكية بواسطة أبل. الهواتف المحمولة كانت منتشرة بطريقة كافية قبل ذلك لكن الهواتف الذكية غيرت الطريقة التي نتواصل بها معا

It is just over a decade since the smartphone was invented by Apple. Mobile phones were common enough before then but the smartphone changes how we communicate with each other.

رقم المكالمات الصوتية عبر الهاتف انخفض لأول مرة في ٢٠١٧ على الرغم من أن الحقيقة أننا معلقين بأجهزتنا.

The number of voice calls made on mobile phones fell for the first time in 2017 - despite the fact we are hooked on our devices.

إجمالي ٧٨٪ من البالغين يمتلك هاتف ذكي الآن.

A total of 78% of all adults now owns a smartphone.

في المتوسط، من المُعتقد أن الناس يتفقدوا هواتفهم كل ١٢ دقيقة عندما يكونوا مستيقظين.

On average, it is believed that people check their phone once every 12 minutes when they're awake.

اثنان من كل خمسة بالغين ينظروا في هواتفهم في خلال ٥ دقائق من الاستيقاظ، والثلاثة يتفقدوا هواتفهم قبل النوم.

Two in five adults look at their phone within five minutes of waking up, and a third check their phones just before falling asleep.

من المعلوم أن نسبة كبيرة (٧١٪) من الناس لا يقوموا بغلق هواتفهم و٧٨٪ يقولون أنّهم لا يمكنهم العيش بدونه.

It is understood that a high percentage (71%) of people never turn off their phone and 78% openly say they cannot live without it.

ثلاثة أرباع الناس يعتبروا المكالمات الصوتية وظيفة هامة لهواتفهم، أكثر من (٩٢٪) يعتقدون أن تصفح الويب ضروري، و يختاروا استخدام هواتفهم في هذا.

Three-quarters of people still regard voice calling as an important function of their phones, more (92%) believe web browsing is crucial, and they choose to use their phone to do this.

من المعتقد أن الرقم الكلي للمكالمات عن طريق الهواتف المحمولة انخفض بنسبة ١.٧٪ في ٢٠١٧، على الرغم من أن المكالمات أصبحت أرخص من اى وقت مضى.

It is believed that the total number of calls made on mobiles fell by 1.7% in 2017, even though making them is the cheapest it has ever been.

هذا لا يعني بالضرورة أن الناس يكلمون بعضهم اقل، لكنهم يفعلون هذا بطرق مختلفة.

That does not necessarily mean people are talking to each other less, but they are talking in different ways.

من المتفق انه، في خلال العقد الماضي، حياة الناس تحولت مع ظهور الهواتف الذكية، مع تحسين فرصة الوصول للانترنت والخدمات الجديدة. يمكننا فعل المزيد أثناء التنقل أكثر من اى وقت مضى.

It is agreed that, over the last decade, people's lives have been transformed by the rise of the smartphone, together with better access to the internet and new services. We can do more on the move than ever before.

اتفق الناس على أن هواتفهم الذكية هي رفيقهم المستمر، لكن البعض يجدوا أنفسهم مشحونون أثناء اتصالهم بالانترنت، أو محبطون عندما لا يكونوا متصلين بالانترنت

People agree their smartphone is their constant companion, but some are finding themselves overloaded when online, or frustrated when they're not.

في داخل العائلات، الأفراد المختلفين يعتمدوا على هواتفهم الذكية لأهداف مختلفة. قد يستخدمه أحدهم لتفقد مواقع التواصل الاجتماعي والجو، ولتخزين قوائم التسوق، وأخر قد يستخدمه لحجز سيارات الأجرة وقراءة البريد الالكتروني. آخرون يستخدموه للعب الألعاب، البحث على الانترنت، ومشاهدة اليوتيوب.

Within families, different members depend on their smartphones for different reasons. One may use it for checking social media and the weather, and to store shopping lists, another will use it to book taxis and read emails. Others use it to play games, search the internet, and watch YouTube.

وبعض العائلات لديهم قوانين عن متى يكون من التهذيب استخدام الهواتف الذكية، ومتى يجب أن تكون مخفية.

And some families have rules for when it is polite to use a smartphone and when it should be kept out of sight.

هل وضعت اى قوانين عن أين ومتى تستخدم هاتفك؟

Have you set any rules for when and where you use your phone?

STORY 15 : CHESTER

القصة ١٥ : شيستر

شيستر هي عاصمة مقاطعة شيشاير، التي تقع في شمال غرب انجلترا، قريبا جدا من الحدود الويلزية. بعض البريطانيين غير متأكدين إذا كانت شيستر في انجلت راو في ويلز، لكنها بالتأكيد في انجلترا.

Chester is the county town of Cheshire, which is in the north-west of England, very close to the Welsh border. Some British people are uncertain whether Chester is in England or Wales, but it is definitely in England.

فضلا عن كونها عاصمة المقاطعة، لقد ظلت مدينة منذ ما يقرب من ٢٠٠٠ عام.

As well as being the county town, it has been a city for nearly 2,000 years.

شيستر مدينة رومانية وما يزال يمكنك رؤية المواقع الرومانية هناك حتى اليوم. أهم هذه المواقع هي أسوار المدينة وهي أكثر أسوار سليمة في بريطانيا. يمكنك بسهولة المشي حول الجدران، هذه الجدران كانت الجدران الأصلية للحصن. كانوا حوالي بطول ٣ كيلو متر وتحيط المدينة الأصلية. تم بنائهم بين ٧٠ ميلاديا و ٨٠ ميلاديا. يمكنك أيضا رؤية بقايا المدرج الروماني. احرص على زيارة متحف التاريخ الروماني حين تكون هناك.

Chester is a Roman town and you can still see many Roman sites there today. The most important of the sites is the City Walls which are the most intact city walls in Britain. You can easily walk around the walls; these were the walls of the original fort. They are about 3km long and surround the original town. They were built between 70 AD and 80 AD. You can also see the remains of a Roman amphitheatre. Make sure you visit the Roman History Museum while you're there.

النهر دي يجري خلال شيستر وهو مركز للإبحار، والتجديف ورحلات القوارب. هي أيضا مناسبة للمشي الطويل والتنزه. الرومان اسموا شيستر ديفا على اسم النهر دي. النهر كان طريق تجاري مهم للرومان وديفا كان لديها ميناء كبير لإحضار البضائع التي تحتاجها المدينة. الميناء لم يعد موجود.

The River Dee runs through Chester and it is a centre for sailing, canoeing, and boat trips. It is also a lovely setting for long walks and picnics. The Romans called Chester Deva after the River Dee. The river was a significant trade route for the Romans and Deva had a large harbour to bring in the goods the city needed. The harbour is no longer there.

بنا قلعة شيستر بدأ في القرن ١١ م، في نفس وقت الكاتدرائية. تم الانتهاء أخيرا من الكاتدرائية في ١٥٣٥ م.

The construction of Chester Castle started in the 11th century AD, at the same time as the cathedral. The cathedral was finally finished in 1535 AD.

ربما تكون شيستر مشهورة بمبانيها البيضاء والسوداء الموجودة فوق بعضها البعض. وهي تسمى "الصفوف". اليوم، تحتوي تلك المباني على مركز تسوق رئيسي وفندق كبير. الجروسفينور.

Chester is perhaps most famous for its black and white buildings which sit on top of each other. They are called 'The Rows'. Today, these contain the main shopping centre and a grand hotel, The Grosvenor.

مركز المدينة مُعلم بصليب، الذي يقع في نقطة التقاء الطرق الرومانية الأساسية.

The centre of the city is marked with a Cross, which stands at the point where the 4 main Roman roads meet.

إذا كنت تريد زيارة مكان مختلف قليلا بكمية هائلة من التاريخ لاستكشافه، فكر في شيستر.

If you want to visit somewhere a little different with a huge amount of history to explore, think of Chester.

إنها جميلة.

It's beautiful.

القصة ١٦ : عطلة عائلية – الجزء ١

STORY 16 : A FAMILY HOLIDAY – PART 1

جلس سارة وبيتر ذات ليلة بكأس من النبيذ. هنري نائم فالسرير وشارلي، الكلب، نائم على الأرض بجوار قدميهما.

Sarah and Peter sit down with a glass of wine one evening. Henry is asleep in bed and Charlie, the dog, is asleep on the floor at their feet.

"هل تريد الذهاب في عطلة هذه السنة" بيتر يسال سارة. "وإذا كنت تريدين، إلى أين تريدين الذهاب؟"

"Do you want to go on holiday this year," Peter asks Sarah. "And if you do, where do you want to go?"

تفكر سارة للحظات وقالت "نعم، سيكون من الجيد الابتعاد. وظيفتي الجديدة ممتازة لكني جاهزة لأخذ استراحة"

Sarah thinks for a few moments and says, "Yes, it will be nice to get away. My new job is great but I am ready for a break."

"إلى أين يجب ان نذهب إذا؟ اى أفكار؟" بيتر يسال مجددا.

"Where shall we go then? Any ideas?" Peter asks again.

كلا منهما اقترح بعض الاقتراحات. اليونان، إيطاليا، البرتغال. ربما ابعد إلى مصر، تونس، تركيا، أو حتى الولايات المتحدة. أو ربما انجلترا؟

They both make some suggestions. Greece, Italy, Portugal. Perhaps further afield to Egypt, Tunisia, Turkey, or even the United States. Or maybe England?

تسال سارة بعدها، "هل يمكننا أن نقرر ما الذي نريد فعله في العطلة قبل أن نقرر إلى أين سنذهب؟ أنا أقصد، يجب علينا أن نفكر في هنري وما الذي سيستمتع به، ليس فقط ما الذي نريد فعله."

Then Sarah asks, "Can we decide what we want to do on holiday before we decide where to go? I mean, we have to think about Henry and what he will enjoy, not just what we want to do."

وافق بيتر قائلا،"حسنا، إذا كان الأمر بيدي، يمكنني أن اذهب واستلقي بجانب شاطئ ما حيث الجو دافئ ومشمس، والذهاب إلى السباحة وشرب الجعة، وعدم الاضطرار لفعل اى مهام منزلية." يضيف "لكن هنري لن يستمتع بهذا، أليس كذلك؟ هو يحتاج إلى أن يكون منشغل ونشط. عزيزتي، لا يمكنني أن أفكر في اى شيء سنستمتع به جميعنا ونستفد."

Peter agrees saying, "Well, if it were up to me, I could just go and lie on a beach somewhere warm and sunny, go swimming, drink beer, and not have to do any house work." The he adds, "But Henry wouldn't enjoy that, would he? He needs to be busy and active. Oh dear, I can't think of anything that we will all enjoy and benefit from."

يجلس كلاهما في صمت ويفكرا فيما يمكنهم فعله لجعل هنري سعيد، وأيضا جعل حياتهم سهلة.

They each sit in silence and consider what they can do that will make Henry happy, and also make their lives easy.

في النهاية، بيتر يصرخ،"ديزني لاند باريس! ماذا عن ديزني لاند باريس؟ دائما نقول أنّنا يجب أن نذهب وأنا اعرف أن هنري سيكون منشغل وسيقضي وقتا رائعا. ماذا تعتقدين؟"

Eventually, Peter shouts out, "Disneyland Paris! What about Disneyland Paris? We always say we should go and I know Henry would be busy and would have a fantastic time. What do you think?"

تلتفت سارة إلى بيتر وتقول، "أعتقد أن هذا سيكون ممتاز. نحن سنكون منشغلين وسنستمتع بوقتنا في نفس الوقت. هنري سيستخدم قدر كبير من طاقته، وستكون تجربة ممتازة لنتذكرها. يا له من اقتراح رائع. لنبدأ في التخطيط!"

Sarah turns to Peter smiling and says, "I think that would be perfect. We would all be busy and having fun at the same time. Henry will use up a lot of his energy, and it will be a great experience to remember. What a great suggestion. Let's start planning!"

STORY 17 : A FAMILY HOLIDAY – PART 2

القصة ١٧ : عطلة عائلية – الجزء ٢

تم اتخاذ القرار،انهم ذاهبون إلى ديزني لاند باريس لقضاء عطلتهم. حان الوقت لبدأ التخطيط.

The decision is made. They're going to Disneyland Paris for their holiday. It's time to start planning.

سارة وبيتر يدخلا إلى الانترنت ليبدأا بالبحث عن ديزني لاند باريس. يبدأا بالبحث عن كيفية الذهاب إلى هناك.

Sarah and Peter go online to start researching Disneyland Paris. They start with how to get there.

يبدوا أن لديهما عدد من الخيارات. يمكنهم اما الطيران ثم اخذ الحافلة، او السفر عن طريق القطار مع بعض التعديلات، أو القيادة هناك بأنفسهم. تعجبهما فكرة القيادة لذلك يقررا أن هذا ما سيفعلونه. هناك العديد من مواقف السيارات لذلك هذا لن يكون مشكلة.

It seems they have a number of options. They can either fly and then take a bus, travel by train with some changes, or drive there themselves. They like the idea of driving so they decide that is what they will do. There is plenty of parking so that won't be a problem.

بدأا في النظر إلى الإقامة وقررا أن الأمر سيكون ممتع أكثر لهنري إذا أقاموا في فنادق ديزني لاند. عندما بدأا يتفقدوها، أدركا إنها مختلفة جدا، وإنها كبيرة جدا. المكوث في واحدة من فنادق المنتجع يعني أنهم يمكنهم أن يمشوا إلى الحديقة كل يوم، لكن، إذا لزم الأمر، يمكنهم ركوب الحافلة في المساء عندما لا تعمل أرجل هنري أكثر من ذلك.

They then start to look at accommodation and decide it will be more fun for Henry if they stay in one of the Disneyland Hotels. When they start looking at them, they realise that they are all very different, and that they're huge. Staying in one of the resort hotels means that they can walk into the park each day but, if necessary, take a bus back in the evening when Henry's legs won't work anymore.

ينظرا إلى الفنادق المختلفة والى انماطها المختلفه. تعجبهم فكرة نيوبورت باي كلوب لكنهم يعتقدوا أن هنري سيفضل فندق شايان لأنه يحب رعاة البقرة والهنود، لذا هوفندق شايان. يتفقدان التواريخ، والتكلفة، والتوفر.

They look at the different hotels and their different themes. They like the look of the Newport Bay Club but think that Henry will prefer the Hotel Cheyenne as he loves cowboys and Indians. So, the Hotel Cheyenne it is. They look at dates, costs, and availability.

ثم يبدأان في التفكير في مدة مكوثهم هناك. بوجود جانبين للمنتزه للزيارة والاستمتاع، لقد بدأا في النظر بالتفصيل فيما يجب فعله بالضبط. الألعاب، العروض، شخصيات لمقابلتها، الجو، وامتصاص المتاح. لقد قررا أن ٣ ليالي وأربع أيام في المنتزه ستكون مناسبة.

They then start to think about how long they will go for. With the 2 sides of the park to visit and enjoy, they start to look in detail at what exactly there is to do. Rides, shows, characters to meet, and the atmosphere to soak up. They decide 3 nights with 4 days in the park will be just right.

لقد كانا على وشك الحجز عندما أدركا أن لديهما شارلي لكي يفكرا بشأنه. ما الذي سيفعلونه بشاري أثناء غيابهم؟ هما لا يعرفان اى أحد يحب الكلاب بدرجة كافية للاعتناء به لاجلهمم، وهم لا يعرفان مربيين للكلاب بالقرب منهم.

They are about to make a booking when they stop and realise that they have Charlie to think about. What will they do with Charlie while they are away? They don't know anybody who likes dogs enough to look after him for them, and they don't know any kennels nearby.

ثم لاحظا أن ديزني لاند باريس لديها مركز للحيوانات الأليفة لحيوانات الزائرين. حل ممتاز – شارلي سيحصل على عطلة أيضا!

Then they notice that Disneyland Paris has a pet centre for the pets of people visiting the park. Perfect solution – Charlie will have a holiday too!

STORY 18 : A FAMILY HOLIDAY – PART 3

القصة ١٨ : عطلة عائلية – الجزء ٣

لقد انطلقوا، وبعد ساعات من التنقل، يخرجوا من الطريق العام ويشقوا طريقهم نحو فندقهم في ديزني لاند باريس. هنري متحمس جدا! شارلي لا يدرك انه يحظى بعطلة أيضا، لكنه متحمس على اى حال.

They set off and after several hours of travelling, they pull off the autoroute and make their way to their hotel at Disneyland Paris. Henry is so excited! Charlie is not aware that he is having a holiday too, but he is excited anyway.

سارة، بيتر وهنري يحجزون داخل فندق شايان ويتركوا شارلي في السيارة لوهلة. الغرفة رائعة وهنري متحمس جدا للنوم في سرير بطابقين. لا يمكنه أن يقرر ما إذا كان سينم في الأعلى أو في الأسفل. يا له من قرار!

Sarah, Peter and Henry book in to the Hotel Cheyenne and leave Charlie in the car for a while. The room is amazing and Henry is very excited to be sleeping in a bunk bed. He can't decide whether to sleep on the top or the bottom bunk. What a decision!

بعد بضع دقائق، قرروا الرجوع إلى السيارة لأخذ شارلي.

After a few minutes, they decide to go back to the car and collect Charlie.

"هل يجب علينا أن نتجه إلى المنتزه الان وتسجيل دخول شارلي في فندقه؟" بيتر يقترح على هنري. يذهبوا إلى المنزه ويجدوا مركز الحيوانات الذي يوجد في موقف سيارات الزائرين. يسجلوا دخول شارلي ويتجهوا إلى المنتزه، مع علمهم انه سيكون سعيد في فندقه أيضا.

"Shall we head to the park now and check Charlie in to his hotel?" Peter suggests to Henry. They go to the park and find the animal centre which is in the visitor parking area. They check Charlie in and head off towards the park, knowing that he will be happy in his hotel too.

يمكنهم سماع موسيقى ديزني السعيدة حولهم ويمشوا بقفزة في خطوتهم. يصلون إلى المدخل الرئيسي ويمروا من فحوصات الحقائب الأمنية.

They can hear the happy Disney music all around them and walk with a spring in their step. They arrive at the main entrance and go through the bag security checks.

ثم يجب عليهم اتخاذ قرار: اما ان يذهبوا إلى المنتزه الرئيسي – منتزه ديزني الأصلي – ولعب العاب ديزني التقليدية، أو الذهاب إلى استوديوهات والت ديزني. يا له من خيار!

Then they have to make a decision: whether to go into the main park - the original Disney Park - and do the traditional Disney rides, or whether to go in to Walt Disney Studios. What a choice!

لذا تسأل سارة هنري، "أين يجب علينا أن نبدأ يا هنري؟"

So, Sarah asks Henry, "Where shall we start, Henry?"

بالنسبة لهنري انه اختيار سهل، "هيا نذهب داخل منتزه ديزني ونبحث عن بعض الشخصيات."

For Henry, it's an easy decision. "Let's go into the Disney Park and look for some characters."

لذا يذهبون إلى ذلك المكان.

So that's where they go.

مباشرة، يروا بلوتو بقرب محطة القطر في بداية الطريق الرئيسي، وهو محاط بأشخاص مبتسمون. يقرروا أن يتخطوه، وفجأة يرون ميكي وميني ماوس يمشيان باتجاههم، هذه المرة لا يوجد حشد من الناس وهنري يجري باتجاههم ليقول مرحبا.

Straightaway, they see Pluto near the railway station at the start of Main Street, and he is surrounded by smiling people. They decide to carry on past him and suddenly see, walking towards them, Mickey and Minnie Mouse. This time, there is no crowd of people and Henry runs towards them to say hello.

ميكي وميني يبتسما ويلوحا ويسلما على هنري. وبيتر يأخذ صورة لثلاثتهم معا. هنري يحكي لهما كل شئ عن شارلي وعن الفندق الذي يقيمون به وميكي وميني يصغيان بإنصات مبتسمين.

Mickey and Minnie smile and wave and 'high five' Henry. And Peter takes a photograph of the three of them together. Henry tells them all about Charlie and the hotel they're stating at and Mickey and Minnie listen with interest, smiling.

هنري متحمس جدا ولا يتوقف عن الكلام.

STORY 19 : A FAMILY HOLIDAY – PART 4

بعد مغامراته مع ميكي وميني ماوس، هنري لا يستطيع أن يقرر ما الذي يريد أن يفعله بعد ذلك، لذلك جلب بيتر خريطة للمنتزه واعطاها له.

After his adventure with Mickey and Minnie Mouse, Henry can't decide what he wants to do next, so Peter picks up a plan of the park and hands it to him.

لنجلس ونرى بالتحديد ما الذي يمكننا فعله، بعد ذلك يمكننا أن نقرر" تقول سارة."

"Let's sit down and see exactly what there is to do. Then we can decide," says Sarah.

هنري يقول انه جائع لذلك يسأل إن كان بامكانهم أن يأكلوا قبل فعل اى شيء أخر. فكرة جيدة.

Henry says he's rather hungry so asks if they can eat before they do anything else. Good idea.

باستخدام الخريطة، نظروا إلى المطاعم المختلفة وهنري وضح انه يريد رقائق البطاطس، وهو لا يمانع ما الذي سيأكله مع البطاطس، لكنه يريد رقائق البطاطس. اختاروا مطعم حيث يمكن لهنري أن يأكل شطيرة مع رقائق البطاطس(شيبسي)، وسارة وبيتر سيتناولون الدجاج والسلطة.

Using the plan, they look at the different restaurants and Henry declares that he wants chips. He doesn't mind what he has with his chips, but he wants chips. They select a restaurant where Henry can have a burger with chips and Sarah and Peter can have chicken and salad.

عندما اشتروا طعامهم، جلسوا وأكلوا ونظروا إلى خريطة المنتزه. الأكل لم يكن طبق فرنسي فاخر لكنه كان جيد جدا.

أنهم يعلمون أنه يجب عليهم الوقوف في الطابور لركوب الألعاب لأنها كانت مزدحمة جدا، لكنهم لاحظوا أنهم بجانب العاب جيدة وأيضا اتفقوا على أن يجربوا لعبة بيتر بان أولا. عندما انتهوا من الطعام، ذهبوا إلى لعبة بيتر بان وانتظروا دورهم.

When they have bought their food, they sit down and eat, and look at the park plan. The food isn't French haute cuisine but it's perfectly fine. They know they will have to queue for the rides as it is so busy, but they realise that they are near to some good rides and so agree to try Peter Pan first. When they finish eating, they walk over to the Peter Pan ride and wait for their turn.

عندما انضموا إلى اللعبة وجلسوا في مقاعدهم، هنري كان متحمس جدا لكن في خلال ثواني معدودة، ذهب في النوم متكئا على سارة مفوتا بقية الجولة. سارة وبيتر قررا انه قد حان الوقت للعودة إلى الفندق والحصول على بعض النوم حتى يكون لديهم طاقة كافية لليوم التالي. اليوم التالي سيكون يوم طويل فيه الكثير من المشي والحماس، لذلك اتفقوا أنهم يحتاجون إلى نوم ليلة جيدة.

When they join the ride and take their seat, Henry is very excited but within just a few seconds, he falls asleep, leaning against Sarah, and misses the rest of the ride. Sarah and Peter decide it's time to go back to the hotel and get some sleep so that they have enough energy for the next day. It will be a long day with lots of walking and lots of excitement, so they agree that they all need a good night's sleep.

حمل بيتر هنري إلى موقف الحافلات، وركبوا الحافلة عائدين إلى فندقهم. وضعوا هنري في السرير بدون أن يستيقظ، ثم جلسوا لكي يرتاحوا. ونظرا في خريطة المنتزه حتى يقررا في اى مكان يبدؤوا غدا، لكنهما اتفقا أنهم متعبين جدا وذهبا إلى النوم.

Peter carries Henry to the bus stop, then they catch the bus back to their hotel. They put Henry to bed without up and sit down themselves to take it all in. They look at the plan of the parks to try to decide where to start tomorrow, but then agree they are too tired, and head to bed themselves.

STORY 20 : A FAMILY HOLIDAY – PART 5

القصة ٢٠ : عطلة عائلية_الجزء ٥

اليوم الثاني من الرحلة إلى ديزني لاند.

Day two of the trip to Disneyland.

استيقظ هنري وهو يشعر انه متعب جدا لكنه كان متحمس جدا. انه حريص على تناول الإفطار مبكرا وبعدها إلى المنتزه. للفطار يختار أن يتناول رقائق الشوكولاتة مع الخبز والمربى وعصير برتقال وشوكولاتة ساخنة ليشربها.

Henry wakes up feeling very tired but very excited. He's keen to go to breakfast early and then into the park. For breakfast he chooses chocolate cereal followed by bread and jam, with orange juice and a hot chocolate to drink.

تمشوا إلى الحديقة مجددا وعلقوا على أن الجو ساخن جدا اليوم. مروا من خلال الأمن مجددا وقرروا أن يأخذوا القطار حول المنتزه حتى يمكنهم رؤية كل شيء موجود هناك. هنري متحمس جدا لرؤية كل هذه الألعاب المختلفة وبدأ بعمل قائمة للألعاب التي يريد أن يذهب إليها.

They walk to the park again and comment that it is very hot today. They go through security again, and decide to take the train around the park so that they can see everything there is to see. Henry is excited to see so many different rides and starts to make a list of the rides he wants to go to.

يقوموا بعمل جولتين اضافيتين في الألعاب قبل أن يقرروا أن يتوقفوا للشرب.

سارة تقول إنها تشعر بأنها ليست بخير -لديها صداع وتشعر بالغثيان -وتحتاج إلى أن تأكل شيءايضا.

يجب عليهم الذهاب إلى الطابور وتبدأ سارة في الهلع ثم أغمى عليها وارتطم رأسها بالأرض.

هنري يبدأ بالبكاء وبيتر ينحني على الأرض بجانب سارة لكي يكلمها ويتفقدها.

بيتر يرى أن لديها جرح في رأسها.

They do two more rides before deciding to stop for a drink. Sarah says she is feeling unwell – she has a headache and feels nauseous - and needs something to eat as well. They have to queue and Sarah starts to panic, faints, and hits her head on the floor. Henry starts to cry and Peter gets on to the floor next to Sarah to talk to her and check on her. He sees she has a cut on her head.

أسرع ثلاثة من العاملين في ديزني لاند للمساعدة وجلبوا مشروبين، ليمون وكوكاكولا وشجعوا سارة على الشرب حتى تتحسن نسبة السكر في دمها.

Three Disneyland staff rush over to help, and bring two drinks, lemonade and Coca-Cola, which they encourage Sarah to drink to help her blood sugar levels.

قامت بشرب الليمون وأعطت الكوكاكولا إلى هنري وتوقف عن البكاء.

She drinks the lemonade and gives the Coca-Cola to Henry, and he stops crying.

ظهر رجل بكرسي متحرك وتم اخذ سارة إلى المركز الطبي ليتم فحصها. الجرح يستمر في النزيف لذلك يقوموا بالترتيب لسارة لكي تذهب إلى أقرب مستشفى لعمل أشعة وخياطة الجرح، وبيتر وهنري ذهبا معها.

A man appears with a wheelchair and Sarah is taken to the medical centre to be checked over. The cut keeps bleeding so they arrange for Sarah to go to the nearest hospital for an X-Ray and stitches, and Peter and Henry go with her.

يتفحصها طبيب في المستشفى سريعا ويتم عمل الكثير من الفحوصات لمعرفة سبب الإغماء. لا يجدوا اى سبب غير كونها ساخنة ومتعبة جدا.

يقوموا بخياطة رأسها وبعد ذلك يرجعوا جميعهم إلى ديزني لاند لاستكمال أجازتهم.

She sees a doctor at the hospital very quickly and has lots of tests to check why she fainted. They do not find a reason, other than her being very hot and very tired. They stitch her head and then they all go back to Disneyland to continue their holiday.

العاملون في ديزني لاند مهتمين جدا وقلقين على سارة وقاموا بعرض وجبة مجانية لهم عندما عادوا إلى المنتزه.

قبلوا الوجبة بامتنان كما انهم جائعون جدا.

The Disneyland staff are very caring and worried about Sarah and offer them a free meal when they are back in the park. They accept gratefully as they are rather hungry.

القصة ٢١ : الوصول للبيت

STORY 21 : GETTING HOME

يحزم كل من بيتر وسارة وهنري أمتعتهم، ويسجلوا خروج من فندق شايان ثم يذهبون ويحضرون تشارلي. يعودون لسيارتهم ويبدءون بالتوجه إلى المنزل بعد رحلتهم الرائعة والمليئة بالأحداث إلى ديزني لاند في باريس

Peter, Sarah and Henry pack their bags, check out of the Hotel Cheyenne, then go and collect Charlie. They walk back to their car and begin to head for home after their fantastic and eventful trip to Disneyland Paris.

إنهم غير متأكدين من الطريق الذي يمكنهم الذهاب اليه لاقصر رحلة للمنزل. إنهم بحاجة لاستخدام الملاحة عبر الأقمار الصناعية لمساعدتهم على القيادة حول باريس ولمعرفة الطريق الصحيح الى المنزل. يحدد بيتر الإحداثيات لعنوانهم وينتظرون توجيهاتهم.

They aren't sure which way to go for the shortest journey home. They need to use satellite navigation (Sat Nav) to help them drive around Paris and to find the right way home. Peter sets the co-ordinates for their address and they wait for their directions.

تقضي الملاحه عبر الأقمار الصناعية بعض الوقت في إيجاد أفضل الطرق.

Sat Nav spends a little time working out the best route.

ثم تقول الملاحه عبر الأقمار الصناعية:

Then Sat Nav says:

سيبدأ التوجيه عندما تلتحق بالطريق المظلل.

The guidance will start when you join the highlighted route.

عندما تصل الى الطريق الرئيسي , التحق بالممر الدائري وخد المخرج الثالث.

When you reach the main road, enter the roundabout and take the third exit.

استمر في السير مباشرة على الطريق السريع لمسافة ١٠ كم.

Continue straight on the motorway for 10 kms.

على مسافة ٥٠٠ متر، عند التقاطع التالي، حافظ على جهة اليمين.

In 500 metres, at the next junction, keep right.

بعد ١٥٠ متر، حافظ علي جهة اليمين والتحق بالطريق السريع.

After 150 metres, keep right and join the motorway.

حافظ علي جهة اليمين.

Keep right.

استمر مباشرة لمسافة ٥ كيلومترات.

Continue straight for 5 kms.

التحق بالممر الدائري وخد المخرج الثاني.

Join the roundabout and take the second exit.

لمسافة ١ كيلومتر، حافظ علي جهة اليسار.

In 1 km, keep left.

التحق بالطريق السريع.

Join the motorway.

الزم الطريق السريع لمسافة ١٠٠ كيلومتر.

Stay on the motorway for 100 kms.

أنت تقترب من كشك رسوم. أبطئ السرعة واجعل تذكرتك جاهزة.

You are approaching a toll booth. Slow down and have your ticket ready.

بعد دفع الرسوم، حافظ على جهة اليسار.

After the toll, keep left.

حافظ علي جهة اليسار.

Keep left.

استمر مباشرة لمسافة ١٠٢ كيلومتر.

Continue straight for 102 kms.

على مسافة ٨٠٠ كيلو متر، خد المخرج.

In 800 metres, take the exit.

بينما تغادر الطريق السريع، حافظ علي جهة اليسار.

As you leave the motorway, keep left.

عند المخرج التالي، حافظ علي جهة اليمين واتبع الطريق لمسافة ٢ كيلومتر.

STORY 21 : GETTING HOME — القصة ٢١ : الوصول للبيت

At the next exit, keep right and follow the road for 2 kms.

لقد وصلت لوجهتك.

You have reached your destination-

عند اقترابهم من نفق القناة، يقومون بتحديد كشك رسوم للدخول.

As they approach the Channel Tunnel, they select a toll booth to approach.

سارة وبيتر قاما بالفعل بالحجز مسبقا واختارا الكشك الآلي، لقد وصلوا مبكرا ويبدون مسرورين لمعرفة أن بإمكانهم أخذ قطاراً أبكر عبر النفق.

Sarah and Peter have pre-booked and select the automated booth. They have arrived early and are pleased to see that they can take an earlier train through the Tunnel.

ينتظرون في المحطة حتى يتم النداء على رمزهم، وشراء بعض السندوتشات لتناول طعام الغداء أثناء انتظارهم.

They wait in the terminal for their letter code to be announced, and buy some sandwiches for lunch while they are waiting.

بعد ١٥ دقيقة، يتم استدعاء رمز حرفهم ويعودون إلى سيارتهم للقيادة إلى القطار والعودة إلى المنزل.

After 15 minutes, their letter code is called and they walk back to their car to drive to the train and the return home.

STORY 22 : OUT SHOPPING AND FOR LUNCH (1)

(القصة ٢٢ : الخروج للتسوق والغداء)١

سارة تشعر إنها أفضل بعد مشكلتها في ديزني لاند باريس.

Sarah is feeling better after her problem at Disneyland Paris.

قبل أن تعود إلى العمل، ترتب لمقابلة صديقة – ناتالي - للغداء.

Before she goes back to work, she arranges to meet a friend – Natalie - for lunch.

تتقابلان في المدينة يوم الجمعة ويذهبان إلى التسوق قبل الغداء.

They meet in town on Friday and go shopping before having lunch.

سارة تقرر إنها تحتاج ملابس جديدة للعمل: بدلة، قميص انيق، فستان، وبالطبع بعض الأحذية الجديدة.

Sarah decides she needs some new clothes for work: a suit, a smart shirt, a dress, and definitely some new shoes.

في البداية تذهبان إلى متجر شامل وتبدءان في البحث عن ملابس مناسبة في أقسام السيدات.

They go first into a large department store and start looking for suitable clothes in the ladies' clothes departments.

سارة تمشي ببطء لكنها لا تجد ما يعجبها. ناتالي تقترح بعض الاقتراحات لكن سارة لازالت غير مهتمة. فجأة، سارة ترى فستان ازرق يعجبها، وتجربه. تقول انه كبير جدا وتسأل عن مقاس أصغر. تسأل أيضا إذا كان متوفرا باللون الأخضر. الأخضر هو لونها المفضل. الفستان ليس متوفر باللون الأخضر، فقط بالأزرق.

Sarah walks around slowly but sees nothing she likes. Natalie makes some suggestions but still Sarah is not interested. Suddenly, she sees a blue dress that she likes, and tries it on. She says it is too big and she asks for a smaller size. She also asks if it is available in green. Green is her favourite colour. It is not available in green, only in blue.

تجرب المقاس الأصغر وتشعر انه صغير جدا لذلك تستمر في البحث.

She tries the smaller size and it feels too small so she keeps looking.

ترى فستان آخر باللون الأزرق الغامق وتجربه. انه صغيراجدا هذه المرة. لذا تسأل عن مقاس أكبر، وهو متاح، بعدها تقوم بتجربته. انه مناسب تماما وناتالي تقول انه يبدوا رائع، لذا سارة تقرر أن تشتريه. ناتالي تقرر أن تجرب الفستان الأزرق السابق وهو يناسبها تماما، لذا تقرر أن تشتريه لنفسها.

She sees another dress in navy blue and tries it on. This time it is too small, so she asks for a larger size, which is available, then tries that on. It fits perfectly and Natalie says it looks great, so Sarah decides to buy it. Natalie decides to try on the blue dress from earlier and it fits her perfectly, so she decides to buy that for herself.

سارة وناتالي تذهبا إلى أقسام مختلفة للبحث عن بدلة مناسبة. سارة لا تستطيع أن تقرر أي لون تريد. تريد أن تشعر إنها انيقة وان ترتدي البدلة على عدد من القمصان المختلفة. ناتالي تقترح أن تبحث سارة عن بدلة رمادية، قائلة أن الرمادي متعدد الاستعمالات ويبدو لائقا مع أي لون.

Sarah and Natalie go to a number of different departments to look for a suitable suit. Sarah can't decide what colour she wants. She wants to feel smart but wants to wear the suit with a number of different tops or shirts. Natalie suggests she look for a grey suit, saying grey is very versatile and goes with any colour.

سارة تكتشف فورا تنوره رمادية تعجبها وتبحث عن معطف بمقاسها لكي يتلائم مع التنورة. عامل المحل يقول أنه ليس لديهم معطف مناسب للتنورة، ويقترح تنوره أخرى تعجب سارة، ولكن ليس بنفس القدر.

Sarah immediately spots a grey skirt she likes and looks for a jacket in her size to go with it. The shop assistant says they do not have a jacket that goes with that skirt, and suggests a different skirt which Sarah likes, but not as much.

سارة محبطة وتسأل ناتالي، "هل أنت جاهزة للغداء بعد؟" أنا أتضور جوعا!"

Sarah is disappointed and asks Natalie, "Are you ready for lunch yet? I'm starving!"

ناتالي سعيدة للذهاب إلى الغداء وتبدءا في التحدث عن مكان الذهاب.

Natalie is happy to go for lunch and they start to talk about where to go.

(القصة ٢٣ : الخروج للتسوق والغداء (٢

STORY 23 : OUT SHOPPING AND FOR LUNCH (2)

سارة وناتالي يتفقان على الذهاب للغداء وتبدءان في التحدث على مكان الذهاب.

Sarah and Natalie agree to go for lunch and start to talk about where to go.

"أنا جائعة جدا،" تقول سارة. "هل تودين بعض الطعام الإيطالي؟ بيتزا أو ربما بعض المعكرونة؟"

"I'm rather hungry," says Sarah. "Would you like some Italian food? A pizza or some pasta perhaps?"

ناتالي ليست متأكدة. "لست متأكدة إذا كنت أريد الطعام الإيطالي. ماذا عن وجبة صينية في مكان ما؟ هل سيكون ذلك جيدا؟"

Natalie is not sure. "I'm not sure I want Italian food. How about a Chinese meal somewhere? Would that be OK?"

سارة محبطة وتقترح شطيرة اللحم ورقائق البطاطس كتسوية. "هل تودين تناول شطيرة لحم(برجر) بدلا من ذلك؟" هي تسأل.

Sarah is disappointed and suggests a burger and chips as a compromise. "Would you like to have a burger instead?" she asks.

"امممم. لست واثقة أني أريد ذلك،" تجيب ناتالي. "تعجبني فكرة رقائق البطاطس لكن ليس شطيرة اللحم."

"Mmmm. I'm not sure I do," answers Natalie. "I like the idea of chips but not the burger."

تفكر كلتاهما في صمت لوهلة.

They both think silently for a while.

"ماذا عن السمك ورقائق البطاطس إذن؟" تسأل سارة.

"What about fish and chips then?" asks Sarah.

"نعم!" تقول ناتالي. "ممتاز!"

"Yes!" says Natalie. "Perfect!"

تذهبا إلى حانة السمك والبطاطس وتطلبا غدائهما. تطلبا ملحا وخلا اضافيان، والمايونيز، والخبز والزبدة ايضا. يا له من غداء ممتاز!

They go to the fish and chip bar and order their lunch. They both ask for extra salt and vinegar, and mayonnaise, as well as bread and butter to go with it. What a perfect lunch!

تشربا الشاي مع السمك والبطاطس وتتحدثا عن تسوقهم.

They drink tea with their fish and chips and chat about their shopping.

سارة تقول أنها محبطة إنها لم تجد البدلة المناسبة. ناتالي تقترح أن ترجعا إلى المتجر لتجريب البدلة التي اقترحها البائع لكن سارة تقول أنها تريد الذهاب إلى مكان آخر.

Sarah says she's disappointed not to have found the right suit. Natalie suggests she go back to the department store to try on the suit the shop assistant suggested but Sarah says she wants to look somewhere else.

تتفقان على الذهاب على متجر مختلف بعد الغداء.

They agree to go to a different shop after lunch.

تمشيان معا وفوراً ترى سارة بدلة رمادية تعجبها. تطلب أن تجربها.

They walk in together and, immediately, Sarah sees a grey suit that she likes. She asks to try it on.

يجد البائع البدلة في مقاس سارة وسارة تجربها. تخرج سارة من غرفة تبديل الملابس وناتالي تقول، "واو!"، متبعة بهذه تناسبك تماما وتبدو رائعة!".

The shop assistant finds the suit in Sarah's size and Sarah tries it on. She walks out of the changing room and Natalie says, "Wow!", followed by, "That fits you perfectly and looks fantastic!".

تشعر سارة بالراحة وتبتسم. وتقرر شرائها وتأخذ بطاقتها الائتمانية من حقيبتها لكي تدفع. تسأل البائع، "كم سعرها؟". تفاجأت وسرت سارة عندما عرفت أن هناك خصم على البدلة وهي تكلف فقط ١٥٠.

Sarah is so relieved and smiles. She decides to buy it and takes her credit card from her purse to pay. She asks the assistant, "How much is that?". She is surprised and pleased to learn the suit is in the sale and only costs €150.

يا لها من صفقة!

What a bargain!

(القصة ٢٤ : الخروج للتسوق والغداء (٣

STORY 24 : OUT SHOPPING AND FOR LUNCH (3)

تشعر سارة شعور جيد عن رحلة تسوقها الان وتبدأ في التفكير بالقميص والحذاء اللذين تريدهما.

Sarah is feeling good about her shopping trip now and starts to think about her shirt and the shoes she wants.

سارة وناتالي ترجعان إلى المتجر الشامل للبحث عن قمصان نسائية وتجدان خيارات عديدة في عدد من الأقسام.

Sarah and Natalie go back to the department store to look for ladies' shirts and find there is a huge choice in a number of departments.

سارة مبهرة بالكمية التي يمكن أن تختار منها وتقرر أنها ستشتري قميصين ليتناسبان مع البدلة الرمادية.

Sarah is amazed how many there are to choose from and decides she will buy two shirts to go with her grey suit.

أولا، تبحث عن قميص أبيض. بسيط وتقليدي. تجد ثلاثة وتجربهم. أحدهم كبير جدا، الأخر صغير جدا، والأخير مناسب تمام عدا أن الأكمام طويلة جدا. تستمر في البحث.

First, she looks for a white shirt. Simple and classic. She finds three and tries them on. One is too big, one is too small, and one fits well except the sleeves are too long. She continues looking.

تجد اثنين آخرين لكنها لا تجد مقاسها في اى منهما. تسأل البائعة إذا كان لديهم مقاسها وتذهب للبحث عنه. ترجع البائعة سعيدة وسارة تجرب القميصين.

She finds two more but can't find her size in one of them. She asks the shop assistant if they have her size and she goes away to find it. She comes back happy, and Sarah tries on the two shirts.

هذه المرة، كليهما مناسبين وسارة لديها قرار صعب لتتخذه. يا للهول! سارة تعرض كلا القميصين على ناتالي وفورا تقول لها ناتالي أيهما تشتري.

This time, they are both perfect and she has a difficult decision to make. Oh dear! Sarah shows both shirts to Natalie and, straightaway, Natalie tells her which one to buy.

سارة توافقها وتبحث عن قميص آخر بلون مختلف. هي تجد نفس القميص في اللون الزهري وتسعد. إذن سارة تشتري قميصين بنفس الطراز، أحدهما ابيض والأخر زهري.

Sarah agrees and then looks for another shirt in a different colour. She finds the same shirt in pink and she is delighted. So, Sarah buys 2 shirts the same style, one in white and one in pink.

Story 24: Out Shopping and For Lunch (3)

ناتالي تذكرها أنهما يبحثان أيضا عن الأحذية، وتتجهان إلى قسم الأحذية.

Natalie reminds her that they are also looking for shoes, and they head for the shoe department.

سارة تقرر أن تبحث عن بعض الأحذية السوداء الانيقة، وناتالي تضيف إنها تريد حذاء ازرق غامق للعمل.

Sarah decides to look for some smart black shoes, and Natalie adds that she wants some navy blue shoes for work.

تجد كلتيهما فورا بعض الأحذية الجلدية الانيقة ويبدو انهم متوفرين باللونين الأزرق الغامق والأسود. تطلبان من البائع مقاسيهما – سارة مقاسها ٣٩ وناتالي مقاسها ٣٧ – ولمفاجئتهما، لدى المتجر مقاسهما باللونين.

They both immediately see some smart leather shoes which seem to be available in both navy blue and black. They ask the assistant for their size – Sarah is a 39 and Natalie is a 37 – and to their surprise, the shop has both sizes in both colours.

تقوما بتجريب لأحذية، وتتمشيا بهم حول القسم لوهلة قصيرة، ثم تقررا شرائهم.

They try them on, walk around the department for a short while, then decide to buy them.

سارة تعود إلى المنزل حاظية بيوم تسوق ناجح جدا وصرف مبلغ كبير من المال. اوه حسنا...

Sarah goes home having had a very successful shopping day and having spent a great deal of money. Oh well...

(القصة ٢٥ : نهاية العطلة (١))

STORY 25 : END OF THE HOLIDAYS (1)

إنه آخر أسبوع في العطلة وبيتر يسأل هنري عما يود أن يفعله.

It is the last week of the holidays and Peter asks Henry what he would like to do.

كل أسبوع، يذهب هنري إلى المخيم الصيفي في المركز الرياضي المحلي ويقول انه يريد فعل ذلك كالمعتاد كما انه يقابل أصدقائه هناك.

Every week, Henry goes to the summer camp in the local sports centre and he says he still wants to do that as usual as he meets his friends there.

بيتر مسرور بهذا الأمر ويوافق. ثم يقوم بعمل بعض الاقتراحات للأيام الأخرى.

Peter is pleased about that and agrees. Then he makes some suggestions for the other days.

"حسنا، يجب علينا أن نشتري لك زي مدرسي جديد ذات يوم، أنا اعرف هذا،" يقول بيتر.

"Well, we need to buy you some new school uniform one day, I know that," says Peter.

هنري يسأل، "هل نستطيع ان نقوم بعمل بعض المخبوزات ذات يوم يا أبي؟ لم نقم بالخبز منذ مدة."

Henry asks, "Can we do some baking one day, Dad? We haven't done baking for ages."

"أنت محق، نحن لم نفعل ذلك،" يوافقه بيتر. "يمكننا أن نخبز كعكة الشوكلاتة وبما بعض البسكويت؟ لكن يجب علينا فعل بعض المهام المنزلية مجددا وان نترك المنزل والحديقة، مرتبين ونظيفين."

"You're right, we haven't," agrees Peter. "We could make a chocolate cake and perhaps some scones? But we need to do some housework again and leave the house, and garden, neat and tidy."

هنري يعلم أن سيساعد في هذا ويأمل انه سيحصل على هدية في النهاية. لكنه أيضا يعلم انه قد لا يحدث لأنه يحصل على مصروف كل أسبوع.

Henry knows he will help with this and hopes he will get a treat at the end. But he also knows he may not because he has pocket money every week.

"لنبدأ بأخذ شارلي للتمشية، هلا فعلنا؟" يقترح بيتر على هنري.

"Let's start by taking Charlie for a walk, shall we?" Peter suggests to Henry.

"هل يمكننا إذا الذهاب إلى الحديقة يا أبي؟" يسأل هنري. هنري يحب اخذ الكرة إلى الحديقة ورميها لشارلي كي يجري لإحضارها.

"Can we go to the park then, Dad?" asks Henry. Henry loves taking a ball to the park and throwing it for Charlie to run after and bring back.

هنري يذهب إلى الأعلى لكي يحضر حذاءه الرياضي لارتدائه للمشي واللعب في الحديقة، بيتر يمسك طوق شارلي. شارلي يعرف على الفور أنهم ذاهبين للتمشية ويصبح متحمس جدا.

Henry goes upstairs to get his trainers to wear for the walk and to play in the park, and Peter picks up Charlie's lead. Charlie knows straightaway that they're going for a walk and is vey excited.

في طريقهم خارج المنزل يلتقطان كرة تينس.

On the way out of the house, they pick up a tennis ball.

يستغرق الأمر خمسة عشر دقيقة للوصول إلى الحديقة. عندما يصلوا إلى هناك، يجدوا أنهم الناس الوحيدين فالحديقة لذلك ليهم مساحة كبيرة للجري واللعب. هنري وشارلي كلاهما متحمس جدا ويلعبا بسعادة لمدة أكثر من ساعة، رمي، ومطاردة، وإمساك، وجلب.

It takes fifteen minutes to get to the park. When they get there, they find they are the only people in the park so they have lots of space to run around and play. Henry and Charlie are both very excited and play happily for more than an hour, throwing, chasing, catching, fetching.

كلاهما مرهق لذا يجلس هنري على أرجوحة وشارلي يستلقي على الأرض بالقرب منه. ينتظروا بضع دقائق قبل أن يمشوا عائدين.

They are both exhausted so Henry sits on a swing and Charlie lies on the ground nearby. They wait a few minutes before they walk back.

في أثناء مشيهم إلى المنزل، يقول هنري، "أبي، أنا اعتقد أن حذائي الرياضي صغير جدا الان. هل يمكننا الذهاب للتسوق للزى المدرسي الجديد غدا ونشتري حذاء رياضي أيضا؟"

As they are walking home, Henry says, "Dad, I think my trainers are too small now. Can we go shopping for my new school uniform tomorrow and buy some trainers as well?"

"نعم يمكننا. فكرة جيدة" يقول بيتر.

"Yes, we can. Good idea," says Peter.

STORY 26 : END OF THE HOLIDAYS (2)

(القصة ٢٦ : نهاية العطلة (٢

في آخر أسبوع من العطلة. بيتر وهنري لديهم قائمة بأشياء لفعلها.

It is the last week of the holidays. Peter and Henry have a list of things to do.

اليوم هو يوم شراء زي مدرسي جديد وخاصة حذاء رياضي جديد.

Today is the day for buying new school uniform and, in particular, new trainers.

بيتر يجد قائمة الزي المدرسي ويبدأ في تفحصها مع هنري. بيتر يقول اسم القطعة، وهنري يجد زي السنة الماضية ويجربه ليرى إذا ما كان لايزال مناسب. اذا لم يكن، ينضم إلى قائمة التسوق. إذا كان لايزال مناسب، جيد، شيء واحد اقل لشرائه.

Peter finds the school uniform list and starts to go through it with Henry. Peter says the item, and Henry finds the uniform from last year and tries it on to see if it still fits. If it doesn't, it goes on the shopping list. If it does, good, one less thing to buy.

بيتر يقول، "هيا نضع حذاء رياضي جديد في أعلى القائمة. نحن نعلم أنهم صغيرين جدا." ويبدءا القائمة.

Peter says, "Let's put new trainers at the top of the list. We know they're too small." And they start the list.

قائمة التسوق:

• الحذاء الرياضي

SHOPPING LIST:

• Trainers

هنري يجرب سرواله القصير وبنطاله، ويجد أن السروال القصير لازال مناسب، لكن السروال أصبح صغير جدا الآن.

Henry tries on his shorts and trousers and finds the shorts fit, but the trousers are too short now.

• حذاء رياضي
• زوجان من السراويل الرمادية الغامقة.

• Trainers
• 2 pairs of dark grey trousers

ثم يجربان قمصان البولو. أصبحوا صغيرين جدا الآن، ويبدوا أنهم رماديين وليسوا بيض، لذا بيتر يضمهم

إلى القائمة أيضا.

Then they try on the polo shirts. They are also too short now, and they look grey rather than white, so Peter adds those to the list as well.

- حذاء رياضي
- زوجان من السراويل الرمادية الغامقة
- ٥ قمصان بولو بيضاء

- Trainers
- 2 pairs of dark grey trousers
- 5 white polo shirts

"أين سترتك يا هنري؟" يسأل بيتر.

"Where is your sweatshirt, Henry?" asks Peter.

"لم اسطع ايجادها في نهاية الفصل الدراسي يا أبي، بالتأكيد احتاج إلى سترة جديدة."

"I couldn't find it at the end of term, Dad. I definitely need a new one."

- حذاء رياضي
- زوجان من السراويل الرمادية الغامقة
- ٥ قمصان بيضاء
- سترة حمراء

- Trainers
- 2 pairs of dark grey trousers
- 5 white polo shirts
- Red sweatshirt

"بالإضافة إلى الحذاء الرياضي، ماذا عن طقم التربية البدنية؟ هل ستحتاج سراويل قصيرة للتربية البدنية؟" يسأل بيتر هنري.

"As well as trainers, what about your PE kit? Do you need any new shorts for PE?" Peter asks Henry.

"سأجربهم"، يجيب هنري. يجد أنهم لازالوا مناسبين، لكنه بحاجة إلى جوارب جديدة.

"I'll try them on," replies Henry. He finds that they still fit, but he needs new PE socks.

- حذاء رياضي
- زوجان من السراويل الرمادية الضيقة
- ٥ قمصان بولو بيضاء.
- سترة حمراء
- جوارب بيضاء

- Trainers
- 2 pairs of dark grey trousers
- 5 white polo shirts
- Red sweatshirt
- White PE socks

"أعتقد أنك تحتاج إلى جوارب رمادية أيضا يا هنري، لذا دعنا نضعهم في القائمة أيضا،" اقترح بيتر.

"I think you need new grey socks as well, Henry, so let's put those on the list as well," Peter suggests.

- حذاء رياضي
- زوجان من السراويل الرمادية الضيقة
- ٥ قمصان بولو بيضاء
- سترة حمراء
- جوارب بيضاء
- ٥ أزواج من الجوارب الرمادية

- Trainers
- 2 pairs of dark grey trousers
- 5 white polo shirts
- Red sweatshirt
- White PE socks
- 5 pairs of grey socks

وفي النهاية، يفكران في حذاء هنري المدرسي. هنري يجربهم ومثل حذائه الرياضي، أصبح صغير جدا، لذا يجب أن ينضم إلى قائمة التسوق.

And finally, they think about Henry's school shoes. Henry tries them on and, like his trainers, they are now too small, so they also need to go on the shopping list.

STORY 26 : END OF THE HOLIDAYS (2) — القصة ٢٦ : نهاية العطلة (٢)

إقتراحات بيتر.

Peter suggests.

- حذاء رياضي
- زوجان من السراويل الرمادية الضيقة
- ٥ قمصان بولو بيضاء
- جوارب بيضاء
- سترة حمراء
- ٥ أزواج من الجوارب الرمادية
- حذاء مدرسي اسود

- Trainers
- 2 pairs of dark grey trousers
- 5 white polo shirts
- Red sweatshirt
- White PE socks
- 5 pairs of grey socks
- Black school shoes

بيتر وهنري يتفقدان القائمة ويتفقان أن أمامهما يوم مشغول من التسوق.

Peter and Henry both look at the list and agree they have a busy day of shopping ahead of them.

STORY 27 : END OF THE HOLIDAYS (3)

(القصة ٢٧ : نهاية العطلة (٣))

مع وجود قائمة التسوق للزي المدرسي، بيتر وهنري يركبان السيارة للقيادة الى المدينة.

With the school uniform shopping list in hand, Peter and Henry get into the car to drive to town.

عندما يصلا، يذهبان أولا لمتجر رياضي لشراء الحذاء الرياضي. هنري يجرب ٤ أحذية مختلفة – أحدهم ابيضا كاملا -والأخر ازرق وابيض، وزوجا منهم احمر وأسود، وأخيرا أبيض واخضر. بيتر يعتقد أن الأزرق والأبيض يبدو أفضل، لكن هنري يريد الأحمر والأسود، لأنه يذكره بفريق كرة القدم المفضل له. الحذاء الأحمر والأسود اغلي، لكن بيتر يوافق عليه.

When they arrive, they go first to a sports shop to buy some trainers. Henry tries on 4 different pairs – one all white pair, one pair that is blue and white, one pair that is red and black, and finally a white and green pair. Peter thinks the blue and white look best but Henry wants the red and black, because they remind him of his favourite football team. They cost more, but Peter agrees to the red and black pair.

بينما هم في المتجر الرياضي، يشتريان لهنري جوارب بيضاء للتربية البدنية.

While they are in the sports shop, they buy Henry's white PE socks.

ثم يذهبان إلى متجر شامل مشهور للبحث عن الخمس قطع الباقية، ومن بينهم الحذاء.

They then go to a well-known department store to look for the other five items, including the shoes.

يجدان القمصان البيضاء فورا وقادران على وضع الخمسة قمصان التي يحتاجها هنري في سلة التسوق. بالقرب من قمصان البولو يوجد سترات بألوان مختلفة: ازرق غامق، أخضر، بنفسجي، أصفر، ولحسن الحظ أحمر. لذا، سترة حمراء مناسبة لمقاس هنري تُوضع في سلة التسوق.

They find the white polo shirts straightaway and are able to put the five shirts Henry needs into the shopping basket. Near to the polo shirts are the sweatshirts in different colours: navy blue, green, purple, yellow and, thankfully, red. So, a red sweatshirt in Henry's size goes into the shopping basket.

الجوارب الرمادية سهلة إيجادها – يوجد الكثير بالمقاس المناسب. خمسة أزواج توضع في سلة التسوق.

The grey socks are just as easy to find – there are plenty in the right size. Five pairs go into the shopping basket.

هناك العديد من السراويل لاختيار منهم أيضا – أو هكذا يعتقد بيتر. يتفقد تقريبا كل سروال على الرف ويجد واحد

القصة ٢٧ : نهاية العطلة (٣)

فقط مناسب لهنري. بيتر يضعهم في سلة التسوق ويحاول أن يجد بائع. لكن بيتر يقرر ألا يقلق لأن هنري سوف يرتدي السراويل القصيرة في أول بضعة أسابيع في المدرسة، ثم أن بإمكانهما طلب سروال قصير عن طريق الانترنت والانتظار حتى يصل.

There are plenty of trousers to choose from as well – or so Peter thinks. He looks at nearly every pair on the racks and only finds one pair that are the right size for Henry. Peter puts them in the basket and tries to find an assistant. But then Peter decides not to worry as Henry will wear shorts for the first few weeks back at school, and they can order a pair online and wait for them to arrive.

يذهبان إلى الخزينة ويدفعان ثمن لأشياء الموجودة في السلة.

They go to the till and pay for the items in the basket.

والان الأحذية. يذهبان إلى قسم الأحذية حيث يوجد العديد من الأحذية للاختيار منهم. بعضهم بأربطة والآخرين بلاصقات. بيتر يقرر أن الأحذية ذات الأربطة أفضل وهنري يجرب حذاء يقول انه مريح جدا. يبدوا انيقا أيضا.لذا، بيتر يدفع ثمن الحذاء أيضا.

And now the shoes. They go to the shoe department where there are many pairs to choose from. Some with laces, some with Velcro straps. Peter decides that laced shoes are better and Henry tries on a pair that he says are really comfortable. They look smart as well. So, Peter pays for the shoes as well.

مع وجود العديد من الحقائب لحملها، بيتر يقترح أن يذهبا لاحتساء مشروب قبل التوجه إلى المنزل. هنري يسأل إن كان بإمكانه أن يأكل شيئا لان التسوق يجعله جائعا.

With lots of bags to carry, Peter suggests they go for a drink before going home. Henry asks if he can have something to eat as shopping makes him hungry.

القهوة والكعك لبيتر، الكولا والكعك لهنري.

Coffee and cake for Peter, Coca-Cola and cake for Henry.

STORY 28 : END OF THE HOLIDAYS (4)

(القصة ٢٨ : نهاية العطلة (٤)

اليوم هو آخر يوم لهنري في المعسكر الصيفي في المركز الرياضي المحلي.

Today is Henry's last day at the Summer Camp in the local sports centre.

عندما يستيقظ، يحزم حقيبته بزي السباحة والمنشفة، ويخرج حذائه الرياضي الجديد.

When he gets up, he packs his bag with his swimming costume and towel, and gets out his new trainers.

يضع طقم كرة القدم والحذاء الرياضي الجديد ويذهب إلى الأسفل لتناول الفطور.

He puts on his football kit and new trainers and goes downstairs for breakfast.

بيتر بالأسفل بالفعل يعد شطيرة لهنري للغداء، ويتحدثان عما سيفعله هنري في المخيم الصيفي.

Peter is downstairs already making Henry's sandwich for lunch, and they talk about what Henry might do today at the summer camp.

"حسنا، نحن دائما نلعب كرة القدم. هذا أفضل جزء. هناك عدد كافي من الناس لست فرق وبعض التبديلات، ونحن نلعب بطولة أثناء اليوم. بين المباريات، يمكننا الذهاب للسباحة أو لعب تينس الريشة،" يشرح هنري.

"Well, we always play football. That's the best part. There are enough people for six teams and a few substitutes, and we play a tournament during the day. In between games, we can go swimming, or play badminton," Henry explains.

"هناك أشياء اخري لفعلها أيضا، نحن نختار" يضيف هنري.

"There are other things to do as well, we choose," Henry adds.

بعد تفكير، يقول،"سأجرب بعض الانشطة المختلفة اليوم، لأنه آخر يوم لي في المعسكر."

Thoughtfully, he says, "I think that I will try some different activities today as well, as it is my last day at camp."

"احب فكرة الرماية،" يقول هنري. "ماذا تعتقد يا أبي؟"

"I like the idea of archery," Henry says. "What do you think, Dad?"

"عظيم. جربها. تبدوا إنها ممتعة. وما هي النشاطات الأخرى المتاحة؟" يسأل بيتر.

"Great. Have a go. It sounds like fun. And what other activities are there to do?" Peter asks.

STORY 28 : END OF THE HOLIDAYS (4) — القصة ٢٨ : نهاية العطلة (٤)

يرد هنري، "حسنا، هناك التجديف في المسبح. لا أعتقد أني أريد فعل هذا. هناك أيضا القفز، وكرة السلة، اعتقد."

Henry replies, "Well, there's canoeing in the swimming pool. I don't think I want to do that though. There's also trampolining, and basketball, I think."

"هل يمكنك فعل جميع الأنشطة إذا أردت ذلك؟" يسأل بيتر هنري.

"Can you do all of the activities if you want to?" Peter asks Henry.

"نعم،" يجاوب هنري، "يجب عليك فقط فعلهم بين مباريات كرة القدم!"

"Yes," Henry answers, "You just have to do them between the football matches!"

يضعا غداء هنري في حقيبته. هنري ينهي فطوره، وينصرفان.

They put Henry's packed lunch into his rucksack. Henry finishes his breakfast, and they leave.

شارلي يبدو حزينا لفكرة قضاء اليوم وحده.

Charlie looks sad at the thought of a day on his own.

بيتر يقود إلى المركز الرياضي، يركن، ويأخذ هنري إلى مكتب التسجيل. هناك العديد من الموظفين هناك أيضا، ويوجد العديد من الأطفال المتحمسين مثل هنري. يبدون سعداء ومتحمسين لرؤية بعضهم البعض وبيتر يعلم أن هنري سيحظى بيوم جميل.

Peter drives to the sports centre, parks, and takes Henry up to the registration desk. There are lots of staff there, as well as lots of energetic children, just like Henry. They look happy and excited to see each other and Peter knows that Henry is going to have a great day.

وبيتر أيضا!

And so is Peter!

STORY 29 : END OF THE HOLIDAYS (5)

(القصة ٢٩ : نهاية العطلة (٥)

هنري في المخيف الصيفي واليوم هو آخر يوم في العطلة حيث يمكن لبيتر أن يفعل ما يحلو له قبل أن يعود للعمل كمدرس الأسبوع القادم.

Henry is at summer camp and today is the last day of the holidays when Peter can do whatever he wants to do before he goes back to work as a teacher next week.

بيتر يأخذ شارلي لجولة طويلة. يذهبان إلى الحديقة ثم يمشيان معا خلال الحقول ويصلان إلى المنزل بعد ثمانية كيلومترات. شارلي يستلقي لغفوة طويلة.

Peter takes Charlie for a long walk. They go to the park and then walk through the fields and arrive home after eight kilometres. Charlie lies down for a long sleep.

بيتر يذهب إلى المطبخ لكي يحضر غداء مبكر ويتوقف ليفكر فيما يريد أن يفعله فعلا أثناء فترة ما بعد الظهيره.

Peter goes into the kitchen to prepare an early lunch and stops to think about what he really wants to do during the afternoon.

ما هي خياراته؟

What are his options?

يمكنه المكوث بالمنزل ومشاهدة التلفاز. لا، يمكنه فعل ذلك وقتما يشاء.

He can stay at home and watch TV. No, he can do that whenever he wants to.

يمكنه الذهاب للتسوق لشراء الطعام للأسبوع القادم. لا، يمكنه التسوق عن طريق الانترنت لشراء الطعام حينما يشاء.

He can go shopping to buy food for next week. No, he can shop online for food whenever he wants to.

يمكنه الذهاب ولعب جولة من الجولف. لا، هو يفضل ان يكون بصحبة أحد ليفعل ذلك، فهو لا يحب اللعب وحيدا.

He can go and play a round of golf. No, he would rather have company to do that, he doesn't like playing on his own.

يمكنه الذهاب للسباحة. لا، هو لا يريد الرجوع إلى المركز الرياضي بعد.

He can go for a swim. No, he doesn't want to go back to the sports centre yet.

يمكنه أن يجز العشب، وينظف المنزل، ويغسل السيارة، وينظف الحمامات. لا، سيفعل ذلك غدا بمساعدة هنري. هذا سيكون ممتعا أكثر.

He can mow the lawn, clean the house, wash the car, and clean the bathrooms. No, he will do that tomorrow with Henry's help. That will be more fun.

يمكنه الذهاب للتسوق وشراء بعض الملابس الجديدة للعمل.

He can go shopping for some new work clothes.

في حقيقة الأمر، هذه ليست فكرة سيئة.

Actually, that isn't a bad idea.

لديه فكرة أخرى. يتصل بسارة.

Then he has another idea. He phones Sarah.

"هل تناولت الغداء حتى الآن؟" يسألها عندما ترد على الهاتف.

"Have you had lunch yet?" he asks her as she answers the phone.

"ليس بعد. أنا اخذ غدائي في حوالي نصف ساعة من الآن،" هي ترد.

"Not yet. I take my lunch in about half an hour," she replies.

"رائع. إذا هيا نتناول الغداء سوياً،" بيتر يقول لها. "أنا قادم للمدينة لكي اشتري بعض الملابس الجديدة. يمكننا أن نحصل على غداء هادئ معا بما أن العطلة على وشك الإنتهاء."

"Fantastic. Let's have lunch together then," Peter says to her. "I'm coming to town to buy some new clothes. We can have a quiet lunch together as my holiday is nearly ovar."

"هذا سيكون جميلا" ردت سارة بإيجاب. "سأقابلك في المطعم الإيطالي في زاوية الشارع الرئيسي. أنا متطلعة إلى ذلك!"

"That would be lovely," Sarah replies, positively. "I will meet you at the Italian restaurant on the corner of the High Street. I am really looking forward to it!"

بيتر مسرور جدا ويسرع إلى الطابق العلوي لكي يغير ملابسه.

Peter is very pleased and runs upstairs to get changed.

STORY 30 : END OF THE HOLIDAYS (6)

بيتر وهنري يتناولان الإفطار سويا في آخر يوم من العطلة. سارة ذهبت إلى العمل مبكرا.

Peter and Henry are having breakfast together on the last day of the holidays. Sarah has gone to work early.

"هنري، اليوم، يجب علينا أن نفعل جميع المهام المنزلية لكي نترك المنزل نظيف ومنظم عندما نرجع إلى المدرسة الأسبوع القادم،" يقول بيتر.

"Henry, today, we need to do all the household jobs so that we leave the house clean and tidy when we go back to school next week," says Peter.

هنري يبتسم ويقول، "أنا اعلم يا أبي، اعلم أن علينا أداء بعض العمل الجاد اليوم. هل نستطيع أن نقوم بعمل بعض المخبوزات بعد أن ننتهي؟"

Henry smiles and says, "I know, Dad. I know we have to do some hard work today. Can we do some baking afterwards though?"

بيتر يوافق على الخبز بعد الظهر عندما ينتهيان من جميع مهامهما المنزلية.

Peter agrees to a baking afternoon when they have finished doing all their jobs.

هنري يعرض أن ينظف السيارة مجددا – هو يستمتع بهذا وفعلها جيدا المرة السابقة.

Henry offers to clean the car again – he enjoyed that and did it well last time.

بيتر يقول له، أولا يجب أن يتأكد أن غرفة نومه منظمة، وان حقيبتة المدرسية مجهزه، وان زيه المدرسي جاهز.

Peter tells him that first, he has to make sure that his bedroom is tidy, his school bag is packed, and his uniform is ready.

هنري ليس سعيد لأنه يجب عليه أن ينظف غرفته، ويذهب إلى الطابق الأعلى ببطء.

Henry isn't happy at having to tidy his bedroom, and goes upstairs slowly.

بيتر يضع الأطباق في غسالة الأطباق، ينظف المطبخ، ثم يمسح أرضية لمطبخ. الآن، المطبخ انتهى نوعا ما.

Peter puts the dishes in the dishwasher, cleans the kitchen, then mops the kitchen floor. Now, the kitchen is more or less done.

بيتر يصعد إلى الطابق العلوي إلى الحمام ليبدأ التنظيف هناك. هو لا يحب تنظيف الحمامات.

Peter then walks upstairs to the bathrooms to start cleaning there. He doesn't like cleaning the bathrooms.

عندما ينتهي من ذلك، يتذكر أن يضع بعض الغسيل في الغسالة. ثم يغير ملاءات السرير.

When he finishes that, he remembers to put some washing in the washing machine. Then he changes the beds.

بيتر يقول لهنري أن عليه الذهاب خارجا لجز العشب. يجده في غرفته ويقول له أن غرفته تبدوا منظمة لذا يمكنه الذهاب وتنظيف السيارة الآن.

Peter tells Henry that he's going outside to mow the lawn. He finds him in his bedroom and tells him that his bedroom is looking tidy so he can go and clean the car now.

بيتر وهنري يذهبان إلى الطابق السفلي معاً. بيتر يجز العشب وهنري ينظف السيارة.

Peter and Henry go downstairs together. Peter mows the lawn and Henry cleans the car.

مجددا يقوم هنري بعمل جيد و السيارة لامعة جدا عندما ينتهي.

Again, Henry does a very good job and the car is very shiny when he finishes.

تبدو الحديقة جميلة عندما ينتهي بيتر أيضا.

The garden looks good when Peter finishes, as well.

يدركان انه وقت الغداء الآن لذا يجلسان معا في الحديقة ويأكلان شطيرة.

They realise it's time for lunch now so they sit down together in the garden and eat a sandwich.

يتأملان بسعادة ما فعلاه هذا الصباح، ويتفقا على أنهما سيقومان بعمل بعض المخبوزات في فترة ما بعد الظهيرة.

They reflect happily on what they have done this morning, and agree that they are going to do some baking in the afternoon.

"ايهما يجب أن نفعله أولا؟ كعكة الشوكلاتة أم البسكويت؟" يسأل بيتر هنري.

"Which shall we make first? The chocolate cake or the scones?" Peter asks Henry.

هنري يفكر للحظة ويقول، "أمي تحب كعكة الشوكلاتة لذا هيا نخبز البسكويت أولا. الكعكة ستكون ساخنة عندما تأتي أمي وستحبها!".

Henry thinks for a moment and says, "Mum loves chocolate cake so let's make the scones first. The cake will be warmer when Mum gets home and she will love it!".

الخاتمة

CONCLUSION

You have just completed the 30 short stories in this book. Congratulations!

We hope that the collection of stories you have read will encourage you to continue learning Arabic. Reading can be one of the best and most enjoyable activities you could do to develop your language skills. Hopefully, you were able to experience that with this book.

If fully consumed as we have intended, these Arabic short stories would widen your Arabic vocabulary and the audio would allow you to follow along to the words, expose you to correct Arabic pronunciation, and help you practice your listening comprehension.

If you need more help with learning Arabic, please visit www.mydailyarabic.com.

Cheers and best of luck to you!

My Daily Arabic Team

تعلميات حول كيفية تحميل التسجيلات الصوتية

INSTRUCTIONS
ON HOW TO DOWNLOAD THE AUDIO

Please take note that the audio are in MP3 format and need to be accessed online. No worries though; it's quite easy! Simply follow the instructions below. It will teach you the steps on where and how to download this book's accompanying audio.

On your computer, smartphone, iphone/ipad or tablet, go to this link:

http://mydailyarabic.com/mp3-arabic-stories/

The link will give you two options:

1. a direct link where you can listen to the audio and download it immediately,

and

2. a link to download the files via Dropbox.

Take note that if you want an easier way to access the files using any type of device (including iOS), choose the direct link option. But if you are a Dropbox user who wants to access the files on your Dropbox account, you can also use the Dropbox option as an alternative.

Here's how to download using the two different options:

Method 1: Get the audio via Direct Link

- In the link provided above, choose the DIRECT LINK option.
- Proceed to the page and listen to the audio directly or download it to any device.

Method 2: Download the audio files via Dropbox

- After selecting the Dropbox option on the page, you will see the MP3 files saved in a Dropbox folder.
- Locate the DOWNLOAD button on the Dropbox folder or save it to your own Dropbox so you can access the audio on connected devices.
- The files you have downloaded would be saved in a .zip file. Simply extract these files from the .zip folder, save to your computer or copy to your preferred devices. If your smartphone or tablet has a zip file extractor, you can download it immediately onto your device.

Do you have any problems downloading the audio? If you do, feel free to send an email to contact@mydailyarabic.com. We'll do our best to assist you, but we would greatly appreciate if you thoroughly review the instructions first.

Thank you.

ABOUT MY DAILY ARABIC

MyDailyArabic.com believes that Arabic can be learned almost painlessly with the help of a learning habit. Through its website and the books and audiobooks that it offers, English language learners are treated to high quality materials that are designed to keep them motivated until they reach their language learning goals.

Keep learning Arabic and enjoy the learning process with books and audio from My Daily Arabic.

Printed in Poland
by Amazon Fulfillment
Poland Sp. z o.o., Wrocław